The Real Reason
Why Christians Are Sick
And How They May Get Well

by Gordon Lindsay

FAITHFUL EDITIONS, LLC
www.faithfuleditions.com
2017

Contents

Chapter	Page

1. SICKNESS VERSUS HEALTH AND PROSPERITY 5
2. SHOULD CHRISTIANS BE SICK? 10
3. WHY ARE CHRISTIANS SICK? 17
4. DISCERNING THE BODY OF CHRIST 22
5. CHRIST'S BODY WAS GIVEN FOR ALL BELIEVERS 27
6. NOT OF HIS BODY? 32
7. SIN IN THE BODY 37
8. SICKNESS AS DISCIPLINE 42
9. SICKNESS AS JUDGMENT 51
10. SATAN'S DESIRE FOR A BODY 55
11. CARE OF THE BODY — EATING "WORTHILY" 60
12. CARE OF THE BODY — REST 66
13. THE BODY IS THE TEMPLE OF THE LORD 70
14. MEMBERS OF ONE BODY 75
15. PAUL'S THORN IN THE FLESH 83
16. CHRIST IS THE HEAD 86
17. PRAYER AND FASTING 90

CHAPTER I

Sickness Versus Health and Prosperity

ARE you one of the many Christians who believes that Jesus has power to heal, and that He has promised healing for you; yet you are sick in body or afflicted with some wasting disease? If so, then this message is for you. While many excellent volumes have been written on the subject of healing, this book so far as we know is the only one in which the entire purpose has been to answer the question, "Why are Christians sick, and what is the remedy?"

To the writer's office flows a vast correspondence from people, many of whom have pitiful stories to tell of lives marred by broken health and sometimes tragedy. Often the story is one of a long train of sickness involving years of suffering. Sometimes it has been of loved ones who in the prime of life have been snatched away, despite the fact that every available dollar was spent for the best of medical skill. In other instances, sickness and misfortune have followed in such unbroken succession as to almost overwhelm the victims with discouragement. Have they prayed? Yes, but alas, their prayers have not been answered. They hope for deliverance, but their faith in the outcome is more of desperation than assurance. They grope blindly on for an answer to their problem.

In these days when thousands upon thousands are receiving wonderful healings, why is it that any should be unable to receive deliverance? Health is a priceless gift while disease and sickness make life so miserable. Why cannot these people be healed? They have prayed and sought the prayers of others. Still they are not delivered. Why should this be?

In answering this question, we realize that for many it involves a matter of life and death. Therefore, we must be frank. We ask, *"Does it not appear that something is fundamentally amiss when people are unable to get their prayers answered?"* The Scriptures clearly indicate that God delights in answering the cries of His people. It is the revealed will of God that His children should experience a life of victory both spiritually and physically. John, the Apostle, who assuredly knew something of the will of God, said in his last epistle, "Beloved, I wish above all things that thou mayest prosper and be in health even as thy soul prospereth." (III John 2).

The 91st Psalm, which most Christians consider one of the greatest chapters of the Bible, bespeaks of the spirit of victory and triumph as normal for the consecrated child of God—the very opposite of despair and defeat. The many promises of Jesus to His followers all indicate that answers to prayer should be the regular experience of all Christians. Christ said, "Ask, and it shall be given you, seek, and ye shall find: knock, and it shall be opened unto you." (Matt. 7:7). Again, He said, "What things soever ye desire, when ye pray, believe ye receive them, and ye shall have them." (Mark 11:24). There are literally scores of Scriptures in the New Testament of similar import. Why is it then that many professed believers find themselves unable to get an answer to their prayers?

Could it be that they have failed in some way to get their lives established upon the whole Word of God? Is it possible that their way of life is out of harmony with the will and purposes of God? Could it be that they are ignorant of God's laws involving the believer's health and prosperity and thus they become peculiarly the target of the devil's malicious attacks? What is the answer to their problem? Where lies its permanent solution? Ah, the answer is simple, but so simple that it is scarcely recognized. What is it? *It lies in the knowledge of the Divine will for one's life, and the willingness to abide in that will.* That is the answer.

When once the human soul is pledged to that course, the powers of Heaven and Earth become its ally and friend. That person will find ere long that circumstances are working in his favor instead of against him. For our God is able to cause "all things (to) work together for good to them that love God, to them who are called according to His purpose." (Romans 8:28). The individual will discover, perhaps to his own amazement, that vexing and insuperable tangles in his life that he despaired of solving, mysteriously begin working themselves out. How is this? Ah—the God Who rules the heavens and causes every star to follow in its appointed path, also rules and overrules circumstances, and is able to cause all to conform to His will.

What is the greatest secret of life? Is it not that *the Creator has a plan for every person born into this world?* God created man in His image. He must surely have a high and noble purpose for him.

Alas, that many are never aware that there is any such plan, and instead seek to fashion their lives to a plan of their own. What a tragedy is a life so spent—a life lived out of the will of God! How sad to contemplate at the journey's end, the thought of "what might have been!" God in His loving mercy and solicitude for the welfare of man ever seeks to interrupt that fateful course. Through sickness, through sorrow, through the failure of fond hopes, through disappointments, caused by man's own erratic choosing, God ever seeks to turn man from his ways unto God's ways. O, that he might read the lesson aright! That he might understand that in man's disappointment is God's appointment!

Why are misfortunes permitted to come upon Christians? The fact is that trouble and sorrow have been the means of bringing many to a place of full obedience to God. The Psalmist says, "Before I was afflicted I went astray; but now have I kept thy word." (Psalms 119:67). There are many illustrations of this working of the providence of God in the lives of man. There was King Manasseh, whose follies and iniquities made his reign notorious above all the kings of Judah. Yet, in his affliction he besought the Lord and repented of his sins. Eventually he was restored to his kingdom. The story of Jacob is a classic illustration of God's dealing with a carnal and self-centered servant. Jonah is another example. He was that foolish prophet who thought to run away from the Lord. It was only when he found himself in desperate circumstances that he remembered to pay his vows unto the Lord. How much better it is to discover God's will for our life without the necessity of the chastening rod!

Is there deliverance for God's people? The answer is, "Yes!" Although God may permit sickness or other misfortune to come to Christians in order to get them to look away from the arm of flesh, and unto Him for help, yet the moment He gets their surrendered will, it is God's delight to heal, to prosper, to pour out upon them blessing in abundant measure, pressed down, shaken together and running over. God has no mysterious purpose to serve, as some mistakenly assume, in allowing His obedient children to suffer in the toils of tormenting sickness, or to endure the bitter pain of loathsome disease. God does not want wretched or unhappy people. But to help them, He must first lead them into a knowledge of His will.

But it is enough. Perhaps the greatest and most universal

of problems confronting Christians is the problem of sickness. Witness the large proportion of believers who seek healing for their bodies. The fact is that altogether too many Christians are sick. To get the answer to why children of the Lord are sick, and, to learn how they may get well, we shall first inquire into that part of the question, "Should Christians be sick?"

Chapter II

Should Christians Be Sick?

IS IT the will of God for the children of the Lord to be afflicted in body? Does God get glory out of their suffering from cruel illness? Is there some mysterious purpose beyond the divination of men, in which God sees fit to lay a vile disease upon His trusting child? In seeking the answer to these all-important questions, let us not be guided by the opinions of men, of which there are many, or by our own personal experiences, which may be varied; but let us go about the matter in the right way. Shall we not inquire, "What saith the Scriptures?" Let God be true though it make every man a liar. True faith can only be builded upon the revelation given us by the Word of God. What the Bible has to say on the question must finally settle the matter. "Forever, O Lord, thy Word is settled in heaven." (Psalms 119:89).

The Bible does not leave us in doubt about the health of God's children. The promises regarding healing are clear and unmistakable. In them we shall see God's will concerning this matter. For the things which were written are for our admonition, as says the Apostle Paul: "Now all these things happened unto them for ensamples: and they are written for our admonition, upon whom the ends of the world are come." (I Cor. 10:11). This verse of Scripture is especially significant, for as we shall see it is of the context which deals with the great reason why many Christians are sick. But ere we consider those remarkable words of the Apostle Paul, let us turn to Exodus 15:26, and see what God had to say about sickness and its relation to His redeemed people:

"There he made for them a statute and an ordinance, and there he proved them. And said, if thou wilt diligently hearken to the voice of the Lord thy God, and wilt do that which is right in his sight, and wilt give ear to his commandments, and keep all his statutes, I will put none of these diseases upon thee, which I have brought upon the Egyptians: for I am the Lord that healeth thee." (Exodus 15:25-26).

Let the reader carefully note the above Scripture. We believe that if it stood alone, it practically answers the question, "Should believers be sick?" Consider the following points:

1. Exodus 15:26 is a promise of healing given to the Children of Israel just after they had passed through the Red Sea. The blood on the doorpost showed that blood having been shed, the death angel would not strike. Israel left Egypt that night and passed through the Red Sea, while Pharaoh and his host following behind were swallowed up in the waters. That was the night of redemption for Israel! Notice the next thing that happened. The Children of Israel came into the wilderness at Marah, where the waters were bitter. In healing the waters of Marah, the Lord gave them a wonderful promise—not only of healing, but of deliverance from sickness altogether!

2. The promise came as a result of Moses' prayer. He cried unto the Lord and the Lord showed him a "tree," which he cast into the waters making them sweet. The "tree" is generally recognized as a symbol of the Cross, thus associating Divine healing with the Atonement of the Cross.

3. The promise of healing was not given as an isolated instance of Divine favor, BUT WAS MADE AN ORDINANCE UNTO THE PEOPLE OF GOD. "There he made for them a statute and an ordinance."

4. Moreover at this time, the Lord revealed one of His redemptive names, "Jehovah Rapha"—"I am the Lord that healeth thee," thus associating healing again with redemption.

5. The most remarkable thing about this promise however, was that if the Children of Israel would hearken unto the Lord, and would obey His statutes, He would (permit) none of these diseases to come upon the Israelites, which had come upon the Egyptians. Thus, more than healing, God had given a greater promise, a promise by which the people were to have immunity from sickness. But note, the promise had a distinct condition attached to it. It was for those only who diligently hearkened unto the Lord and obeyed His commandments and statutes.

The promise of Exodus 15:26 is plain and its meaning unmistakable. Nevertheless, some do not accept it. They say this promise was given to the Children of Israel and is therefore not applicable today. How odd that such a statement should be made. What strange interpreting of the Old Testament to deny its promises of blessings and then lay claim to its curses. At Marah, healing was considered a blessing from the Lord, while the 28th chapter of Deuteronomy tells us that sickness is a curse. Those who would think of sickness as a blessing from God should carefully read that chapter. Notice that in it God lists a long catalogue of diseases which were to come upon Israel *if she were disobedient*.

Lest any should fail to understand the meaning of the promise given in the Scripture just mentioned, the Lord repeats it in Exodus 23:25. Why is the promise repeated unless God should attach great importance to it?

"And ye shall serve the Lord your God, and he shall bless thy bread, and thy water, and I will take sickness away from the midst of thee."

Notice, that this is not a mere promise of Divine healing, but it involved the removing of the curse of sickness from the very midst of God's people. The food that they ate, and the water that they drank would be blessed, and their bodies would be well and strong to glorify God. But again, there is a condition attached to the promise—*it was for those that served the Lord.*

The book of Deuteronomy is a summary of the law of God. Is the promise of immunity from sickness repeated there? It is. For the third time the promise is repeated. "A threefold cord is not quickly broken." (Eccl. 4:12).

"And the Lord will take away from thee all sickness, and will put none of the evil diseases of Egypt, which thou knowest, upon thee; but will lay them upon all them that hate thee." (Deut. 7:15).

Here are some things worthy of notice. First, that God promised to take away, not some sickness, but *all sickness.* Next, disease is called an *evil thing.* This refutes the idea advanced by some that sickness is a "love token" from the Lord which He places upon His obedient children to bless them. Rather the implication is that sickness was for the disobedient. Notice also that this promise was given in connection with an injunction that the people of God were to be an holy people, a separate people, a chosen people. "For thou art an holy people unto the Lord thy God; the Lord thy God hath chosen thee to be a special people unto himself, above all people that are upon the face of the earth ... know therefore that the Lord thy God, he is God, the faithful God, which keepeth covenant and mercy with them that love and keep his commandments to a thousand generations." (Deut. 7:6, 9). We again see that with the promise there are certain well-defined conditions that go with it.

Was this promise practical? Did the Children of Israel enjoy its blessings? They did as long as they obeyed the Lord. During their journey in the wilderness, the Psalmist says, "There was not one feeble person among their tribes." (Psa. 105:37).

But what about the New Testament? Are there any such promises there? Let us say that there is not the slightest suggestion that either the apostles or Christ were ever sick. We do know that when Paul was stoned at Lystra, and the disciples stood about him supposing he was in a dying condition, he picked himself up and went on to his next preaching appointment. The apostle's explanation of this mystery is no doubt found in his words in Romans 8:11: "But if the Spirit of him that raised up Jesus from the dead dwell in you, he that raised up Christ from the dead shall also quicken your mortal bodies by his Spirit that dwelleth in you." This apostle expresses the will of God when he speaks about the body, as well as the soul and the Spirit, being preserved blameless until the coming of the Lord. "And the very God of peace sanctify you wholly; and I pray God your whole spirit and soul and body be preserved blameless unto the coming of our Lord Jesus Christ." (I Thes. 5:23).

There are many other passages in the Scriptures indicating that the will of God for the believer is that he should have a healthy body. But perhaps the most impressive of these is the statement which we have quoted before, made by the Apostle John when he was nearing the close of his ministry:

"Beloved, I wish above all things that thou mayest prosper and be in health, even as thy soul prospereth." (III John 2).

Here John expresses his wishes to the elder Caius, that above all things he desired that he should prosper and be in health. But again blessing is qualified with a condition. The condition is that prosperity and health should be in that proportion that the soul prospers. If the soul were not to prosper, it would infer that the health of the body might not prosper. Health and prosperity for the Christian, according to the Scriptures, apparently had a direct relation to the prosperity of the soul.

This, then, is the Bible picture. Both in the Old Testament and in the New, the direct teaching is that the obedient child of God should have deliverance not only over sickness but from sickness. Nor are these Scriptures contrary to experience. In the great revivals now spreading over the land, healings and miracles are taking place beyond number and count. Many Christians have learned to enjoy this health that is promised. Every kind of disease is disappearing before the mighty Name of the Lord Jesus Christ.

The world has become aware that something is transpiring in its midst. Audiences of ten, twenty-five and even seventy-five thousand do not gather at a gospel meeting without a purpose. Perhaps one of the most startling developments is the number of people in heathen lands who are receiving healing. Likewise, in our country many who have come to evangelical meetings for the first time in their lives, have also received glorious deliverance. These great things that are taking place are stirring the multitudes as never before.

Still there is one thing that is puzzling to many. There are sincere Christians of good standing in practically every church who apparently fail to receive healing. Some of these have been prayed for time after time, but their condition is not much improved. Why is this? Why may a sinner cry out, "God be merciful to me a sinner" and get saved and healed, often by a startling miracle, while some Christians who have attended the house of God for years, fail to receive? This seems to be paradoxical and confusing. It is a question that is asked time and again. It is indeed a question to which countless children of the Lord are anxiously seeking the answer. Strange though it may seem to some, the Bible does give the complete answer. The Word of God informs us exactly why Christians are sick. Our difficulty has been that instead of carefully looking to the Scripture, we have looked for the answer elsewhere. Thus we have failed to find it.

Therefore the problem of sickness among believers has not been satisfactorily solved. It is to supply this answer in such a way that every Christian who is sick may understand the cause of his sickness and how he may remove that cause, that these pages are written.

Chapter III

Why Are Christians Sick?

NOW to the great question, "Why are Christians sick?" We have seen according to the 28th chapter of Deuteronomy that sickness is not a blessing but a curse. We have also seen that it is the will of God that Christians should be well and strong. Why then are many of them sick?

It is true that God may get glory out of a sickness, but only in the fact that the person is healed of it. Jesus said that the sickness of Lazarus was for the glory of God, but God got no glory until Lazarus was raised up. When Lazarus died, there was only sorrow and despair. Indeed Martha and Mary almost reproached the Savior when they said, "Lord, if thou hadst been here, my brother had not died." (John 11:21, 32). It was when Lazarus was raised from death that many came to believe in the Lord.

Sickness is not a blessing but a curse. It has the touch of the devil upon it. Disease is loathsome and of the pit. What is so repulsive as a vile cancer that eats the life out of a person? Sickness often causes people to become deeply discouraged and many have lost their minds as a result of it. Although there are notable exceptions, it is observable that a chronic invalid tends to become self-centered and peevish— not more spiritual as is sometimes claimed. Sickness is no respecter of persons. It may cut a mother off from her little brood just when she is so urgently needed to protect and care for them. Who can hear the heartbreaking cry of little children who have lost one or both of their parents through some dread stroke of illness, and not realize what a curse it is?

What then is the cause of sickness among Christians? We refer not to its origin, for we know that it is the direct work of the devil. It was Satan who laid the painful boils on Job. (Job 2:7). It was Satan who bound the daughter of Abraham, whom Christ loosed on the Sabbath day. (Luke 13:16). It was Satan who oppressed God's people whom Jesus went about healing. (Acts 10:38).

If sickness then is the curse of the devil, why is it that Christians are sick? Why should they be subject to a curse? There must be a cause, for the Scriptures declare, "The curse causeless shall not come." (Prov. 26:2).

Many have been the explanations of the cause of sickness among Christians. Mainly the basic cause has been overlooked. In certain cases the reasons advanced are decidedly unscriptural. For example, it has been claimed that Christians often suffer in their body for the glory of God. Others assume that sickness is in the natural order of things, and therefore to be expected. To them it is the matter of finding the most skillful physician or surgeon they can afford and then praying that he will administer the right medicine, or wield the scalpel just right. Not a few are of the opinion that if the evangelist who prays for them has sufficient faith, they will be healed regardless of any other circumstance that may exist. Still others resignedly believe that they are suffering for some mysterious reason that is inscrutable and unknowable. The list of opinions expressed on this subject is almost endless. It is not strange that the one great Scriptural explanation as to why Christians are sick, has been passed almost unnoticed?

Let us turn to the Word of God for an answer to this all-important question. We shall expect a straightforward answer, one that plainly tells us why Christians are sick, and one that explains how they may get well. Is there such an answer in the Bible? Or, has God in preparing His perfect revelation for man, overlooked this one important matter? We assure the seeker that regarding this vital need, as well as every other need of the believer, God has not only made ample provision, but has given a complete revelation in the matter. It is not God's plan that His children remain in doubt. He has given a full answer. We shall now consider it:

"For he that eateth and drinketh unworthily, eateth and drinketh damnation to himself, not discerning the Lord's body. For this cause many are weak and sickly among you, and many sleep." (I Cor. 11:29, 30).

There it is! There is the cause! We are told that many are weak, many are sickly, many sleep—that is have died before their time—why?—because they do not discern the Lord's Body. In this brief statement is bound up the whole answer to the problem of why Christians are sick, and as God is true, here also is shown the remedy. Here we shall find the clue as to how the believer may put an end forever to sickness and disease in his life.

Let us observe carefully the meaning of the above Scripture. Paul was telling the Corinthians that many of their number partook of the Communion unworthily. As an example, he said, some looked upon the Lord's Supper as a mere social event. These shallow Christians seemed to have no sense of realization that those sacred elements that they partook of so lightly, represented the very body and blood of the Lord Jesus Christ! They thus ate unworthily, and brought judgment upon themselves. They failed to discern in the Holy Communion, that in truth, they were partaking of the body of the Lord Jesus Christ.

Yet that is the meaning of the Communion. Let us follow the matter closely for it leads us to the great truth of healing and health. The cup and broken bread of the Communion, answer to the very body of the Lord, sacrificed at Calvary, as a ransom for many. It was in memory of Christ's death, in atonement for mankind, that the Lord's Supper was instituted. Paul calls this to their mind in the familiar passage of I Corinthians 11:23-26:

"For I have received of the Lord that which also I delivered unto you, that the Lord Jesus the same night in which he was betrayed took bread: And when he had given thanks, he brake it, and said, Take, eat: this is my body, which is broken for you: this do in remembrance of me. After the same manner also he took the cup, when he had supped, saying, This cup is the new testament in my blood: this do ye, as oft as ye drink it, in remembrance of me. For as oft as ye eat this bread, and drink this cup, ye do shew the Lord's death till he come."

Most Christians understand the matter thus far, but the significance which naturally follows is not understood. It is in that which follows that is revealed the great secret of a Christian's health. Strange that most of us have missed it so long. Let us see what it is:

"The cup of blessing which we bless, is it not the communion of the blood of Christ? The bread which we break, is it not the communion of the body of Christ? For we being many are one bread, and one body: for we are all partakers of that one bread." (I Cor. 10:16, 17).

Here is the secret! The partaking of the Communion is an outward symbol of a strange and wonderful work of God. In so many words we are told *that as we partake of the bread of Christ, we become members of the Body of Christ* —that is, we as members of His Church also become members of His Body! Christ is the Head, we are the members. Paul gives the entire 12th chapter of I Corinthians to explaining this vital truth. He says, "Now ye are the Body of Christ, and members in particular." (I Cor. 12:27). Paul

Why Are Christians Sick? 21

further explains about how we become members of this Body in I Corinthians 12:12-14:

"For as the Body is one, and hath many members, and all the members of that one Body, being many, are one Body; so also is Christ. For by one Spirit are we all baptized into one Body, whether we be Jews or Gentiles, whether we be bond or free: and have been all made to drink into one Spirit. For the Body is not one member, but many."

There is no new doctrine here. Jesus preached a whole sermon on this subject in John 6. The evangelical Church believes this truth—yet the vast significance of it has been lost. And because it has been lost or overlooked, many believers are sick.

The realization of the fact that by virtue of partaking of Christ we become members of the Lord's Body gives us a completely new approach to the subject of the Christian's health. Our bodies are not our own! We are members of His Body, and subject to the law of Christ. As a man should know at least something about his physical body if he is to preserve his health, so we being members of the Body of Christ must know something about that Body and the laws which govern it, if we are to have health. In fact, the whole matter of sickness and health in the Church revolves around this fact. It is a great truth and in understanding it lies our health and prosperity. Let us get the significance of it. The reason that Christians are weak and sickly is because they do not discern the Lord's Body. According to this, the supposition that believers are sick for some mysterious reason in the providence of God, or that they are suffering for the glory of God, is erroneous. Christians are members of the Body of Christ and as such, Paul said, "I pray God your whole spirit and soul and body be preserved blameless unto the coming of our Lord Jesus Christ." (I Thes. 5:23). In our next chapter let us see just what discerning the Lord's Body means, and its relation to our health.

Chapter IV

Discerning the Body of Christ

"And when he had given thanks, he brake it, and said, Take, eat: this is my body, which is broken for you: this do in remembrance of me. After the same manner also he took the cup, when he had supped, saying, This cup is the new testament in my blood: this do ye, as oft as ye drink it, in remembrance of me. For as often as ye eat this bread, and drink this cup, ye do shew the Lord's death till he come. . . . For he that eateth and drinketh unworthily, eateth and drinketh damnation to himself, not discerning the Lord's body. For this cause many are weak and sickly among you, and many sleep." (I Cor. 11:24-26, 29, 30).

WE ARE now considering the meaning of the words of Paul which he spoke in I Cor. 11:29-31. What does it mean to discern the body of Christ? The Communion of the cup, as every Christian knows is a symbol of the blood of Christ which He shed for many for the remission of sins. It is important for the believer to understand the meaning of the cup which he partakes. Paul gave special instructions regarding the partaking of the Holy Communion. In I Corinthians 10:20, 21, he declares that a Christian must lead a separated life, that he cannot be a partaker of the Lord's table and the table of devils. The Lord's Supper should be observed with reverence and holy respect. (I Cor. 11:20-22). In other words those who partake of the Communion of the cup should understand its meaning and discern that it represents the blood of Christ which was shed for them. Without the shedding of blood there is no remission of sins. Most devout Christians understand this. Some, however, do not accept nor discern that the shedding of Christ's blood purchased salvation. Because of this it can do them no good.

But this is not all. At the same Communion the believer takes also of the broken bread, which is a symbol of the broken body of the Lord. For the Lord said, "Take, eat: this is my body which is broken for you." What significance has the broken bread from that of the cup? Now the sad thing is that many have no idea of the meaning of the broken bread. This ignorance can have tragic results, just as ignorance of the meaning of the cup can have serious consequences. For the apostle says that he that eateth and drinketh unworthily, not discerning the Lord's body, may be subject to sickness, and may even die before his time.

What does it mean to discern the Lord's body of the Communion? What is the significance of the broken bread? Is it not that as we partake by faith we become an actual part of the body of Christ? "For we are members of his body, of his flesh, and of his bones." (Eph. 5:30). In becoming part of the body of Christ, sickness should have no more mastery over us than it had over the body of Christ when He was on earth. As one recognizes this truth he may be said to have discerned the Lord's body. While the majority of the Church does understand and does discern the blood of Christ and its power to heal the believer of his sins, *yet nevertheless, many do not discern the body of Christ and its power to heal their diseases.* They do not discern and understand that as they partake of Christ they become part of the body of Christ and therefore should not be subject to sickness, any more than Christ was subject.

The fact that Divine Healing is in the Atonement of Christ is prefigured in the covenant of healing which God gave to the Children of Israel at the waters of Marah. As we have observed, when the Lord gave to the people the ordinance of healing, as a sign He asked Moses to take a "tree" which He showed him and to cast it into the waters—and the waters were made sweet. This "tree" as the Scofield Bible brings out in its notes, is the Cross. Galations 3:13 declares that "Christ hath redeemed us from the curse of the law, being made a curse for us: for it is written, Cursed is everyone that hangeth on a tree." It is certainly significant that the Lord should associate the Cross with the granting of the Covenant of healing to Israel and the revelation to Israel of His name, "Jehovah Rapha, I am the Lord that healeth thee." *The significance is that Divine Healing is in the Atonement.*

The prophet Isaiah in his beautiful chapter depicting the sufferings of the Messiah declares in Isaiah 53:5, "And with his stripes we are healed." *Notice the present tense.* Isaiah lived over 600 years before Christ, but he could say even in that day that the Atonement of Christ brought healing those many centuries before that time. Isaiah knew what he was talking about. He was not ignorant of the ministry of healing. When Hezekiah was sick unto death and there was not an earthly hope for his recovery, Isaiah carried God's message to the king saying, "Thus saith the Lord, the God of David thy father, I have heard thy prayer, I have seen thy tears: behold, I will heal thee: on the third day thou shalt go up unto the house of the Lord. And I will add unto thy days fifteen years. . . ." (II Kings 20:5, 6). Peter, looking back to the Cross, could change the tense and say, "by whose stripes ye were healed." (I Peter 2:24). The healing for the Christian has already been accomplished—just as salvation has already been accomplished. Actually a Christian should not find it necessary to search for healing, he should be enjoying the health of the body of Christ. He will—if he truly discerns that he is a member of the body of Christ.

Discerning the Body of Christ

The prophet Isaiah had yet further to say about healing being in the Atonement of Christ. Let us note how Matthew quoted from it in Matt. 8:14-17:

"And when Jesus was come into Peter's house, he saw his wife's mother laid, and sick of a fever. And he touched her hand, and the fever left her: and she arose, and ministered unto them. When the even was come, they brought unto him many that were possessed with devils: and he cast out the spirits with his word, and healed all that were sick: That it might be fulfilled which was spoken by Esaias the prophet, saying, Himself took our infirmities, and bare our sicknesses."

The above is one of the most important Scriptures bearing on the subject of healing in the Bible. Jesus had healed Peter's mother-in-law. Inspired by this manifestation of healing power, at eventime the people of Capernaum brought to him a great multitude of sick people, some possessed of devils, and others afflicted with diseases. Jesus healed them all—not some of them—"That it might be fulfilled which was spoken by Esaias the prophet, saying, Himself took our infirmities, and bare our sicknesses." It is impossible to mistake the import of this Scripture. Men might have interpreted Isaiah differently, but Matthew interpreted it to mean that *the reason that Jesus healed all the people that came to Him was because He had already taken their infirmities and borne their sicknesses!*

Now if Christ has already borne our sickness once, there is certainly no need for us to bear it the second time. It is apparent that sickness has no more right to have dominion over our body than sin. Of course we know that unless we look to Christ in faith, the sins that Christ delivered us from will still have dominion over us, even though Christ is the Lamb of God that taketh away the sin of the world. (John 1:29). Likewise although the Lord has borne our diseases, sickness may still have dominion over us unless we rise up and appropriate that which has been purchased for us. We must discern the blood of Christ for the remission of our sins and the healing of our soul. We must also discern the broken body of Christ for the healing of our body.

Why are Christians sick? Simply because they do not discern the Lord's body which was broken for their bodies. Therefore in the taking of the Communion, we should partake in faith, knowing that we are partaking of His flesh, and that in so doing we become bone of His bone and flesh of His flesh. As members of His body, neither sickness nor sin should have any more dominion over us than it had over the body of Christ.

Chapter V

Christ's Body Was Given for All Believers

IN THE preceding chapter we have seen how that Christ took the sickness of His people upon Himself. Now if you are a Christian and are still sick, then it is well to proceed step by step and watch carefully to discover at just what point the trouble lies. Perhaps you are not absolutely sure that it is God's will to heal you. This can effectively keep you from getting healed. A sinner who stumbles in doubt and does not know whether it is God's will to save him, stays in darkness until he can be persuaded that it is God's will. So it is that those who are not certain whether it is the will of God to heal them, effectually cut themselves off from healing. We must settle that matter once and for all, just as every believer settled the matter of Christ's willingness to save when they were converted. The fact is that just as the blood of Christ was given to save the soul of every sinner, so Christ's body was broken for the healing of the body of every believer. Let us notice how this great truth is revealed in the Brazen Serpent in the wilderness, which is one of the types of Christ.

The Children of Israel were on their way to the Promised Land. They had learned many lessons while they were wandering in the wilderness. Nevertheless they had not gotten victory over some things. They complained because of the manna, which did not entirely satisfy them. Then came the plague of fiery serpents, which bit the people so that many of them died from the poison. The Children of Israel repented of their sin and sought God for a remedy. Moses prayed for the people and the Lord instructed him to prepare a Serpent of Brass and to place it upon a pole. All who were bitten by the fiery serpent would, if they looked upon the Brazen Serpent, live. But it was necessary to look; if they did not look, the victims died.

In this we see an important truth, and one reason that some people are not healed. Suppose a person bitten by a serpent said, "Well I'm depending on Moses' prayer. If he has faith I will get well." What would have happened? The sick person would have died. Suppose he should have said, "I know that healing is for others, but I don't think it will work for me. It's no use for me to look." It would have happened just as he expected it would. Or if he had thought, "Well, it's not convenient for me to go over where the Brazen Serpent is, and if God wants to heal me, He'll heal me here," he would have surely died. It was necessary to *look* at the Serpent, if the person were to be healed.

What has this lesson to do with us today, and the fact that many people are not healed? Notice that the Brazen Serpent is a type of Christ. Jesus, just before He spoke the words of John 3:16, referred to the Serpent in the wilderness. He said that as the serpent was lifted up, so He, Christ, must be lifted up. "And as Moses lifted up the serpent in the wilderness, even so must the Son of Man be lifted up." (John 3:14). Here is surely one of the strangest types of Christ—a Brazen Serpent! This type involves one of the most awesome aspects of the Redemption, the fact that Christ was made sin for us! "For he hath made him to be sin for us, who knew no sin." (II Cor. 5:21).

Now the truth plainly taught here is two-fold. First, that as all who looked upon the Brazen Serpent were healed, so all who look upon Christ will receive deliverance for their soul. This is one of the most glorious truths of salvation! However, we must not restrict this deliverance as to mean healing for the soul only. It must also include healing of the body. *Odd indeed it would be, that if all who were dying from the serpents' bites, should look upon the Brazen Serpent and be healed, yet those who look upon Christ should not all be healed!* What strange theology is this that would admit the antitype had power to heal all, and Christ Who is the reality that the type points to, should not have that power! Nay, but all who will look upon Him may be healed of whatever may be their sickness or affliction.

And now let us notice something which follows, that is of great significance and which explains why many are not healed. In the days of the Reformation, there was a teaching that was widely advocated—the teaching of the "limited atonement." By that term it was meant that Christ's death was efficacious for *a limited number of the elect,* whom it was God's will to save. The others, no matter how much they desired salvation, could not be saved. What was the effect of this doctrine? It destroyed faith. Millions came to suppose that they were not of the elect and could not be saved. The spirit of revival was quenched and apostacy set in. For according to this doctrine it was no use for men to look upon Christ Who was made sin for them—for since they might not be of the elect, it would do them no good. Then came Wesley and Finney. They refused to accept the doctrine of the "limited atonement," and opposed it, pointing out that the Bible taught that the Lord desired all men to come to repentance. They declared that all could be saved, if only they would turn from their sins and look to Christ. What was the result? God honored their preaching, great revivals broke out and multiplied thousands were saved. Out of their preaching came the spiritual awakenings of the Eighteenth and Nineteenth Centuries.

Today most of the evangelical churches accept the doctrine of the unlimited power of Christ to save. It has been proven too many times that the Lord is willing to save all. But the devil never gives up. Today he is busy getting people to believe that there is a "limited atonement" as far as Divine healing is concerned. So we are told by some that Christ's Atonement is limited in the matter of healing of the body. That healing is for a certain few, and not for the rest. Thus, people are discouraged to look to Christ in faith for healing. And just as unbelief caused many to fail to receive salvation, so unbelief causes many to fail to receive healing. Just as those in Moses' day who were bitten by the serpents, and refused to look upon the Brazen Serpent, died, even so today, many who fail to look to Christ as providing healing for them, succumb to their sickness.

Let us see how this effects us. The Brazen Serpent is a type of the stricken body of Christ, when He bore the sin and sickness of the world. If we fail to discern that body —a body broken for our body—if we fail to discern that the body of Christ is as the Brazen Serpent, able to heal not only a few but all, then we may fail to get our healing. It was no use to say in Moses' time, "If God wants to heal me, He'll heal me; no need to bother about looking at the Brazen Serpent." With that attitude the person would die. If we say today, "Divine healing may not be for all; better not be too sure that Christ will heal us if we look to Him," then the same result will take place. We must discern the body of Christ. We must discern that His body was broken for our body. We must surely believe that as all who looked at the Brazen Serpent were healed, so all who discern the body of Christ of which the Serpent is the type, will also be healed. For again we repeat that surely it would be strange that the type had power to heal all, while the Person of Whom it was the type, had power to heal only some.

Is it God's will to heal all? We dare not guess at this. If the Bible declares that healing is only for certain favored ones, then we must accept it as so. But what has God's word said? Does it not say that we are to bless the Lord "and forget not all his benefits: Who forgiveth all thine inquities; who healeth *all* thy diseases?" (Psa. 103:2). God has expressed His will in His word, therefore we dare not doubt. We must discern that the Christ Who was lifted up on the Cross, has not only carried our sins but also borne our diseases. Failure to understand this truth may result in our being weak and sickly. Let us settle this matter once and for all as we settled it in the matter of the salvation of our soul. His body was broken for our bodies that we might be healed.

Forever, in heaven, is God's word settled. At Capernaum Christ healed all that were brought to Him, whether possessed of devils or afflicted with diseases, "that it might be fulfilled which was spoken by Esaias . . . Himself took our infirmities, and bare our sicknesses." Why did Christ, that evening at Capernaum, heal all that were brought to Him? Because He had borne the sickness of all, not just a part of the people. Therefore He healed all. Many of these people that evening had learned of Christ for the first time. Yet they were healed. How much more those that are members of His body should be healed.

CHAPTER VI

Not of His Body?

THE graciousness of God is infinite and beyond comprehension. When a man comes to Him, sick and sinful and asking for Christ's deliverance, God takes the man at his word, heals him, and accepts him, trusting that the man henceforth will live for and serve Him. Yes, God has fully provided for the sinner who stands humbly at His door. The penitent may not be worthy of the "children's bread," but in asking for crumbs, Christ in His love often gives him a double portion.

There are however, those who have entered the door of the church who have never repented of their sins. They have therefore never been truly converted to Christ. They yet love the world and their heart is not single before God. They have partaken of the Communion of Christ but they have done so unworthily. Instead of a blessing, the Communion has become to them a curse. Because they are not converted, though they are in the church, they are not of the church. They have not become members of His body. Many such people become sick, and, seeing that the Lord heals others, they too seek healing. Such people, however, are outside the pale of the promise. Divine healing is the "children's bread." It is for members of the body of Christ. They must come humbly and receive healing for their soul as well as for the body.

The Church is the Body of Christ. Israel in the wilderness was a type of that Church, and was called the church in the wilderness. (Acts 7:38.) We are told in I Corinthians 10:1-6 that the things that happened to Israel in the wilderness were for example. Now it is clear that Israel's passage through the Red Sea answers to, and is a type of God's redemption of His people. *Notice that the promise of healing and health was not given to Israel until they had been redeemed!* Afterwards they were given an ordinance that if they obeyed the Lord and gave heed to His statutes, none of the diseases of Egypt would come upon them, and that from henceforth the Lord was to be their Healer. But Israel was given this promise only after she was redeemed.

Healing and health is for the Body of Christ and the members thereof. This has been freely provided through God's plan of redemption. Although God through His sovereign grace may heal an ignorant sinner whose heart is open to Him, God has given no promise of healing for those who resist His grace and refuse to be members of His Body. Actually, many church members have never been born again, and therefore are not members of the Body of Christ. We are not of Christ until we have partaken of Christ. (I Cor. 10:16.) When we partake of Christ by faith, in other words become converted, then the Spirit of God sets us into the Body. (I Cor. 12:13.)

Here is an important reason that some are not healed. They have joined some religious organization supposing that this saves them. But there has been no repentance before God, no breaking up of their hearts to let Him in their life. Thus, they are not members of the Body of Christ. They have therefore no grounds to expect healing.

Fortunately for us all, God is compassionate and looks down in pity upon our ignorance. Those who come to Him ignorantly, He seeks to help; but they must let Him help them. He must deal with them frankly. Some people deeply resent being dealt with plainly about their spiritual condition. Yet Christ did not hesitate to deal truly with all that came to him.

There was the case of the Syrophenician woman. (Matt. 15:21-28.) This woman had about everything happen to her that could discourage a seeker for healing. She had a daughter that was demon-possessed, and as far as human help was concerned, there was no chance that the girl would get better. The woman was a Gentile, therefore not of the commonwealth of Israel, and to her no promises were given. She came to the Lord and presented her petition for help, but at first the Lord "answered her not a word." (Matt. 15:23.) The disciples were for sending her away, but she persisted. Then the Lord said, "I am not sent but unto the lost sheep of the house of Israel." (Vs. 24.) Still the woman refused to leave Him, and worshipping Him, plead, "Lord, help me." (Vs. 25.) Then came the crowning rebuff. Jesus said, "It is not meet to take the *children's bread* and cast it to dogs." (Vs. 26.) There seemed to be no further use for hope on her part. But despite all these discouragements, the woman showed an astonishing faith, and accepting the position of a dog, asked for the crumbs.

Now through it all Christ loved her and pitied her, though she was not on healing ground. She was a Gentile and outside the Kingdom but Christ led her on, until she confessed Him not as the Son of David but as Lord, and, in deep humility admitted her unworthiness. She acknowledged that she had no claim on God save through His grace and mercy, and in so doing she got on healing ground! And her daughter was healed!

The great truth revealed here is that Divine healing is "the children's bread." Those who have not given their heart to God, those who have refused to consecrate their life to the Lord, have no proper claim on Him. Some would bargain with God, and say, "If He will heal me, I'll serve Him."

They must be willing to listen patiently, and to learn the way of salvation. Then they can be healed. Alas, that many come to be healed who are not willing to let Christ be their Lord. They ask for a blessing with one hand, and reject blessings with the other hand. We cannot reject and accept blessings at the same time.

The Psalmist showed the connection between salvation and Divine healing when he said, "Bless the Lord, O my soul; and all that is within me, bless his holy name. Bless the Lord, O my soul, and forget not all his benefits; who forgiveth all thine iniquities; who healeth all thy diseases." (Psa. 103:1-3.) Divine healing is there. We are admonished not to forget or ignore it. But forgiveness and salvation precede the promise of healing.

Time and again Jesus sought to show that forgiveness of sin was associated with the work of healing. On one occasion they brought a man that was sick of the palsy to him. Jesus, seeing their faith, said unto the sick of the palsy, "Son, be of good cheer; thy sins be forgiven thee." Later He told the man to take up his bed and walk. The man's sins were forgiven and he was healed at the same hour.

Naaman is another illustration of God's dealing with the soul of man before He healed the body. Naaman was a leper and had come all the way from Syria to be healed. He was a general, a brave man, a man in a position of honor and authority. He supposed that Elisha in healing him, would strike his hand toward heaven, and command the leper to be healed. But instead the man of God commanded him to do a very humbling thing. Naaman was told to go and dip himself in the River Jordan seven times. He was so taken aback by this unexpected reception that he turned away in a rage. But after receiving some good advice from his servants, he reconsidered and decided to obey the prophet's command. Naaman was healed! He returned to tell Elisha that from then on he would worship Jehovah Who was the only true and living God. Had God healed him at the first, the chances are that his spirit would have been unhumbled and he would have gone back to Syria without God.

These things are a lesson to us. Divine healing is the "children's bread." In partaking of the bread of Christ, we partake of His body and become a member of His Body. "Flesh of his flesh and bone of his bones." We cannot truly receive of this bread unless we are willing to become one with Christ.

> "The bread which we break, is it not the communion of the body of Christ? For we being many are one bread, and one body: for we are all partakers of that one bread." (I Cor. 10:16, 17.)

LESSON: Divine healing is the children's bread and only promised to those who are a part of the Body of Christ. We must discern that Body as the Body of the Lord and by faith become a part of it. As a member of the Body of Christ, sickness has no more right over us than it had over the body of the Lord when He walked on Earth.

Chapter VII

Sin in the Body

THE subject of our last chapter leads us directly to another matter. In the last chapter we have considered the results of ignorance. Now Paul would call our attention to the result of wilful violation of the laws which govern the Body of Christ.

"Wherefore whosoever shall eat this bread, and drink this cup of the Lord, unworthily, shall be guilty of the body and blood of the Lord. But let a man examine himself, and so let him eat of that bread, and drink of that cup. *For he that eateth and drinketh unworthily, eateth and drinketh damnation to himself,* not discerning the Lord's body. For this cause many are weak and sickly among you, and many sleep." (I Cor. 11:27-30.)

In the Early Church even as it is true today, there was the problem of sickness. In the Corinthian Church the problem was especially acute. Many were sickly and many had died before their time. The Church believed in healing, indeed had the gifts in its midst, but deliverance for many had not come. Doubtless skeptics said as they do today, "If Divine healing is the will of God, why don't those people get healed?" Skeptics have changed very little.

Paul acknowledged that sickness was in the Church. He did not say that it ought to be there. He did not say that the sick people were glorifying God with their sickness. He said that there was a cause for it; that the people were partaking of Christ unworthily and bringing judgment upon themselves. Furthermore he said that they should examine themselves and find out what was wrong.

Let us see what this means. In the beginning God created man, and intended him to live in perfect health. Then sin came into the world, and following it came sickness and death. Sin and sickness are concomitants. Try to solve the problem of sickness without solving the problem of sin is a fatal mistake. For sin and sickness are sisters and go hand in hand together.

In partaking of Christ we partake of His life and His health. But in partaking of Christ, we must not repeat the disobedience of Adam. We are no longer of the old body of Adam but of the Body of the Second Adam. If we continue to sin we shall find that Christ's power shall not avail in our life.

The fact that we profess to be Christians, yet do not seem to be able to get our healing is a warning signal. It may mean that through ignorance we have not appropriated the promises of God for our healing. It may also mean that sin is in our life, or in some way we are out of harmony with God. In the ordinance relating to prayer for the sick as recorded in the Book of James, it will be noted that the writer assumes the possibility that the sick person may have committed sin. He says, "And the prayer of faith shall save the sick, and the Lord shall raise him up; and if he have committed sins, they shall be forgiven him. Confess your faults one to another, and pray one for another, that ye may be healed." (James 5:15, 16).

The poison of sin may be working in a person's life, and yet he expects healing and wonders why it does not come. Obviously one must get rid of the poison before he can expect a cure. When sickness comes to a Christian he should carefully examine his life. "But let a man examine himself." If he has been harsh, unforgiving, careless, disobedient in his Christian walk, let him examine himself, and confess his sin before he asks for healing. The command is to confess our faults and our sins and pray one for another that we may be healed. The fact that James suggests that sin may be involved in the sickness of a believer is of vital significance. The individual should confess his sin and turn from it. God is gracious and will forgive and heal.

The forgiveness of sin and the healing of the body are often associated in the Scriptures. Thus we read of the Psalmist who, blessing God for his benefits, says:

"Bless the Lord, O my soul, and forget not all his benefits: who forgiveth all thine iniquities: who healeth all thy diseases." (Psa. 103:2, 3).

As we have noted previously, when Jesus met the man sick of the palsy he sajd, "Son, be of good cheer; thy sins be forgiven thee." (Matt. 9:2). Then He commanded the man to arise and walk. Thus the Lord showed the relation of the forgiveness of sins with the healing of the body.

There was another man whom He also told to arise and walk. That was the lame man at the pool of Bethesda. (John 5:8, 9). Suppose the healed man continued in his sins; what then? The Lord's answer to this possibility is significant. He said, "Behold, thou are made whole: sin no more, lest a worse thing come unto thee." (John 5:14). Thus we are told in the solemn words of the Lord Jesus Christ that after we are saved and healed, if we yet continue in sin, we can expect a worse thing to come upon us. No subterfuge may explain away this solemn warning.

This truth is taught in Luke 11:24-26. Jesus had healed a dumb man by casting out the devil. Then He gives a warning. He explains that the devil who is cast out goeth "through dry places, seeking rest; and finding none." At last the devil decides to go back to the "house" where he had been cast out. He finds it swept and garnished. The devil takes with him seven devils more wicked than himself and returns and the last state of that man is worse than the first.

The fact that sin can bring sickness is a truth that is taught throughout the Scriptures. Failure to get rid of that sin is an effectual hindrance to an individual's healing. Alas how often it is true, that a person is committing some sin that may seriously block his growth in God, yet he is complacent about his condition and quite unaware of his spiritual poverty. Samson lived a carnal life, and "wist not that the Lord was departed from him." (Judg. 16:20).

Paul indicated that some were drinking of the cup of the Lord unworthily and seemed to be unaware of it. He said that those who drank of the cup should examine themselves. "For if we would judge ourselves, we should not be judged." (I Cor. 11:31). In other words when a man who professes to be a Christian, finds that a sickness has come upon him, it is time for him to examine himself and find the cause.

Here is where many people make their mistake. When they get sick they cannot imagine that there is any cause for their illness. Their only thought is to get someone to pray for them. Now this is only partly right. The sick are commanded to call for the elders of the church to pray the prayer of faith. (James 5:14). But the same Scripture advises that they be ready to confess and forsake their sins. The first and most important thing for a sick person to do is to examine himself in the light of the Word of God, and see what is the cause of the sickness that has come upon him. When he has done this, it usually is not difficult for him to get deliverance.

However, it is true, as we shall see, that sickness is not always caused by sin. There are other causes. It may be caused by failure to properly care for the body, or by neglect in giving it the right food and sufficient rest. This we shall consider elsewhere. But there is a cause and we should find out what it is.

Sin in the Body

We repeat, the Christian is a member of the Communion of Christ. As such he shares the sacred privilege of partaking of the bread and the cup. But if he takes the matter lightly, and continues to live a careless worldly life, he fails to realize the seriousness of his calling. He fails to discern the Lord's Body, that he is a member of that Body. He fails to see that those to whom is given the great privilege of partaking of the body of the Lord must walk holy before Him. Failing this, sickness and disease may come to plague him.

Let the sick person therefore, consecrate his life afresh to Christ. Let him separate himself from all known wrongdoing, either by commission or omission. Let him examine himself, so that he does not eat and drink "damnation to himself, not discerning the Lord's body."

Some have a terrific battle to surrender all to Christ. They have some pet sin they cannot give up, some lust which they wish to indulge in. Without a great crisis they will not give it up. People at times get into a place where preaching has no effect on them, and they tend to justify themselves in their indulgences. When sickness comes and the alternatives of life and death become very real, these same people may be brought to a place of renewed consecration to God, and in many cases are willing to give up the follies that are leading them away from Christ.

Our bodies are members of the body of Christ. We must yield them to the Spirit of God and not to the spirit of this world. We must never take our body which is a temple of the Holy Ghost into an unholy place. A certain woman who was a professing Christian broke her leg in a theater. She was thus on the devil's territory at the moment of her accident. Whenever we yield our bodies to sin or unrighteousness, we get on the devil's territory, and become vulnerable to the attacks of the enemy.

Chapter VIII

Sickness as Discipline

"For this cause many are weak and sickly among you, and many sleep. For if we would judge ourselves, we should not be judged. But when we are judged, we are chastened of the Lord, that we should not be condemned with the world." (I Cor. 11:30-32).

IN THE last chapter we have seen how the sins of omission and commission can affect the health of the Christian. In the above verse we see how the phrase "chastened of the Lord," is directly associated with sickness in the believer's body. We should distinguish carefully between sickness as involving a chastening of the believer, and affliction that comes as a direct result of wilful sin. Some Christians suffer because they have deliberately violated the law of God. One such obvious case is recorded in I Cor. 5:1-5. In this chapter, however, we are particularly interested in sickness as it may involve the disciplining of the children of God, to lead them to an understanding of God's will for their life to the end that they might be healed without further delay.

We were told in Exodus 15:26, that if God's people desire to be free from disease and sickness they should diligently hearken unto the Word of God and obey His laws and precepts. In the New Testament, the great truth that we are asked to give attention to in relation to healing is the one directing us to discern the Lord's Body. Our proper conduct in this wonderful relationship is a matter of the utmost importance to our physical welfare. Failure to discern the Lord's Body may result in weakness and sickness and even death.

Some turn from their carelessness only when they see death approaching. Often at such a time the person has been led to seek the Lord earnestly. Although sickness very definitely is a means in the providence of God of awakening people from their carelessness, how much better it would be for them to be led by the Lord gently, rather than of necessity or by stern measures.

Man ever seeks to justify himself! When sickness comes, not a few, instead of examining their lives and seeking to establish themselves more firmly on the Rock, like to think that they are suffering for the glory of God! Such is a comfortable thought to the human ego, but such false reasoning seriously hinders people from receiving deliverance. Certainly Paul held no such view. He associated sickness and physical weakness among Christians as a condition indicating the possibility of divine chastening.

A classic scriptural illustration of the subject we are considering is the story of Job. In the account of the sufferings of this patriarch we learn many things concerning God's providential dealings with His people. One thing that we should understand from the beginning regarding Job is the circumstances under which he became sick. This will help us to understand just what is meant by sickness being associated with the chastening of God. Notice this fact particularly: God did not make Job sick nor put the boils upon him. God only *permitted* the sickness to come. It was the devil that put the boils on Job. True, the devil tried to give the impression that God touched Job with disease. He said, "But put forth thine hand now, and touch his bone and his flesh, and he will curse thee to thy face." (Job 2:5). The devil would like to have people believe that God did satan's own dirty work. But the devil lied when he made this inference. God exposed the lie by recording in Job 2:7, "So went Satan forth from the presence of the Lord, and smote Job with sore boils from the sole of his foot unto his crown." Strange that some people still believe the devil's lie. Far from putting the boils on Job, God actually prevented the devil from killing him, which he would like to have done. "And the Lord said unto Satan, Behold, he is in thine hand: but save his life." (Vs. 6). Poor Job, when he was suffering, didn't realize what was really happening. He said, "The Lord gave, and the Lord hath taken away; blessed be the name of the Lord." (Job 1:21). Actually the Lord had given but the devil had taken away.

But it is contended that there are some passages in the Bible that would indicate that God, Himself, directly put diseases on people, such as in II Chron. 21:18. Such statements are to be only understood in the permissive sense. In Romans 8:32 we are told that God "spared not his own Son, but delivered him up for us all." Does this mean that God killed His own Son? Such an interpretation would be blasphemy. God did not kill His own Son, but in order to save the world, He did permit others to do it. Ungodly men, inspired by the devil, took Christ and with wicked hands slew him. (Acts 2:23 and Luke 22:53). God did permit His Son to die at the hands of Satan-inspired men. He also permits the devil to put diseases upon His people. In both cases He permits these things to happen, as incidental to the fulfillment of His purposes.

Dr. Young, author of the great Analytical Concordance that bears his name, points out in his "Hints and Helps to Bible Interpretation" that Exodus 15:26 has been translated in the causative sense when it should have been translated in the permissive sense, and shows that it should read,

"I will permit to be put upon thee none of the diseases which I have permitted to be brought upon the Egyptians; for I am the Lord that healeth thee."

Actually the devil would destroy all of God's people with disease if he could. The reason he does not is because God has set up a hedge of protection, through which Satan cannot penetrate. The devil had been hoping to get at Job for a long time. He wanted to destroy him, to take his life if possible. But because of God's protection, he could not get to him. As a matter of fact, the devil complained to God concerning this very matter, saying, "Hast not thou made an hedge about him, and about his house, and about all that he hath on every side? Thou hast blessed the work of his hands, and his substance is increased in the land." (Job 1:10). The truth is that instead of God's putting disease on people, He sets up a hedge of protection which keeps the devil from doing it. God does, however, under certain circumstances permit the enemy to put diseases upon the people of God. What these circumstances are is plainly explained in the Bible. Nevertheless, it hurts spiritual pride to admit that sickness is caused by the devil. Therefore many people flatter themselves by claiming that they are suffering for the glory of God.

But it is claimed that Job was a perfect man, and was called so by the Lord. How is this? Why did God allow a perfect man to become afflicted by a disease of the devil? In answering this question we touch on one of the most wonderful truths of God's plan of redemption. God reserves the right to chasten His people, but He will not allow the devil to slander them. Though God's people have erred, yet if they are humble and accept His pardon, His redemptive grace covers their sins, and God sees them positionally perfect before Him.

We would make a great mistake, however, if we interpreted Job's perfection as sinless perfection. This is so evident that it hardly requires proof. God spoke also of Noah as a man who was "perfect in his generations." (Gen. 6:9). Yet Noah on one occasion became drunk with wine. (Gen. 9:23). Obviously the Scripture's use of the word "perfect," indicates the best that God can expect of a man under the conditions. Noah was perfect in his generations, that is, as good a man as God could expect under the circumstances of his time, and so God reckoned it. God is not an unreasonable God, and does not exact more from man than he can give. He is indeed gracious. Just as obvious, however, is the fact that God is not satisfied that the spiritual condition of His people remains at a static level, and in His providence, He ever seeks to draw them closer to Himself, and to make them like Himself. Even Job came to know that God was working this process in his life, for he said, "But he knoweth the way that I take: when he hath tried me, I shall come forth as gold." (Job 23:10).

It is true that God was fulfilling an important purpose in demonstrating to Satan and all subjects of Earth, Heaven and Hell that there were those who, like Job, would serve Him regardless of the fires of trial and tribulation they went through. But we miss a significant truth in the story of Job, if we assume that God afflicted Job just merely to prove something to the devil, and that God had no beneficent purpose for His child.

Was Job sinlessly perfect? It is a fact that many of the charges of his friends were false. They did not get at the root of the matter at all. They assumed that because Job was sick, that he had some terrible hidden sin in his life. They were off the track, and later had to ask Job's forgiveness. This is a lesson to those who would indiscriminately charge sick people with hidden and gross sin. Such accusers often find that it is not long before they, like the false comforters of Job, are called by God for a personal accounting of themselves. Yet although we may not harshly condemn the sick, and at all times must conduct ourselves sympathetically toward them, this does not mean that we are not to teach them the ways of truth, and indeed must do so if they are to be healed. Therefore, since almost all Christians have been attacked by sickness at some time or another, there are lessons that all of us may well learn. These lessons are not to be restricted to a certain few.

The facts are that more than one thing was impeding Job's walk with God, although he was quite unconscious of these things. He was not committing known sin, nor was he guilty of conscious transgression. His most glaring fault was self-righteousness. He was righteous in his own eyes. (Job 32:1). When people become convinced of their own goodness, it is often difficult to convince them of their error. Job said, "I am clean without transgression, I am innocent; neither is there iniquity in me." (Job 33:9).

A leaning toward self-righteousness can definitely keep a Christian from receiving his healing. The way to deliverance from affliction is by the road of humility and a due appreciation of our own unworthiness. There is no possibility of receiving healing on our own merits.

Notice that sickness, itself, does little in the way of purifying people, as is sometimes claimed. Chronically sick people often become more cantankerous, the longer they are ill. The longer Job was sick, the more selfrighteous he became. However, *it did result in his seeking God*. As he was brought face to face with God and His righteousness, he then realized how far his attitude had been from what God desired of Him.

Where else had Job erred? For one thing, he married a woman whose ideals were utterly contrary to his own. When Job's misfortunes came upon him, she suggested that he blaspheme God. Said she, "Dost thou still retain thine integrity? curse God, and die." (Job 2:9). Of course Job rebuked this impious suggestion. But why did a man who had such great knowledge of Jehovah, marry a woman totally void of spiritual grace in the first place? Had he been led away by her beauty? Job's wife raised him a set of ungodly children, and they were busy wining and dining when the cyclone struck. It may be pointed out, as having some bearing on this matter, that Job continually prayed for his children. True, and we are certain that eternity will show that his prayers were answered. But obedience is always better than sacrifice. The results of some of our errors cannot be easily rectified in this world. One of these is a marriage to an unbeliever. Perhaps it was these things that were responsible for the fear that was in Job's life. He was afraid; he anticipated trouble ahead—a day of reckoning. Fear is an open door through which the enemy may attack us. Thus when the stroke came, he lamented: "For the thing which I greatly feared is come upon me, and that which I was afraid of is come unto me. I was not in safety, neither had I rest, neither was I quiet; yet trouble came." (Job 3:25, 26). It is a sin to fear, not a gross sin in the sense of some kinds, but it is a distrust in God's providence, a lack of faith in the Divine goodness. Fear is an emotion that provides a perfect opening for the approach of sickness. Fear breaks down the hedge that God has set up to protect us from the attacks of the enemy. Jesus often said to His disciples, "Fear not." "Do not be afraid." Again the Scripture declares, "For God hath not given us the spirit of fear; but of power, and of love, and of a sound mind." (II Tim. 1:7).

The vital truth, however, in the story of Job is that he got healed! To hear many people talk you would suppose that Job were sick all his life, and finally died while scraping himself with a potsherd among the ashes. The fact is that the time that he was ill was perhaps only for a few weeks.

He lived after that 140 years. Job was healed as soon as he came to understand God's will and providence for his life. When he got a fresh vision of God and His majesty, his self-righteousness fled, and in its place appeared a deep humility. No longer did he proclaim his righteousness, but said, "Behold, I am vile . . . I abhor myself, and repent in dust and ashes." (Job 40:4; 42;6). Note one more thing: Job was healed, not when he was praying for himself, but when he prayed for his friends, who had condemned him so unmercifully. (Job 42:7-10).

Job lived apparently before the Law was given, for he says nothing of it in his long discussions concerning the providence of God. Undoubtedly he lived before the promise of healing had been given. Nevertheless, he was healed. His day was many centuries before the Church, consequently he was not of those believers that make up the Body of Christ. No doubt sickness has always been an indirect means in the providence of God, of drawing His people into a closer walk with Him. Sickness in itself does not make a man better, but like a danger signal, it brings one to attention. Through sickness, God often gets a person's attention which He could not get otherwise.

We who live with a full revelation of God's Word, have the benefit of many promises that Job did not have. It should not be necessary for us to be sick as long as Job was. Paul declares, "For if we judge ourselves we should not be judged. But when we are judged we are chastened of the Lord." (I Cor. 11:31, 32). If we judge ourselves, correct our errors, understand what is required of us, that is, understand that we are members of the Lord's Body, it should not be necessary for us to be sick. God will get far more glory in our being well and serving Him.

Let us repeat that sickness, among God's people has a cause. If we judge ourselves, that is, correct the things that are wrong in our lives, if we recognize that we are members of the Body of Christ and conduct ourselves in a way that will bring honor to the Church of God, then we no longer have need of discipline. God has no desire that those who have learned their lesson be chastened for the sake of chastening.

In no sense was the sickness that came upon Job, punishment. It was disciplinary, and out of his trials came a new understanding of the will of God in his life. His healing was definite and lasting. There is such a thing, however, of sickness being judgment, and we shall notice this fact in the next chapter.

CHAPTER IX

Sickness as Judgment

> "For he that eateth and drinketh unworthily, eateth and drinketh damnation to himself, not discerning the Lord's body. For this cause many are weak and sickly among you, and many sleep. For if we would judge ourselves, we should not be judged." (I Cor. 11:29-31).

WE HAVE seen how sickness may come as Divine discipline. Now we shall observe how it actually comes in judgment upon some who have sinned against light and have committed crimes against God and man. There is such a thing as judgment coming upon people who deliberately outrage the grace and mercy of God.

In the case of Ananias and Sapphira, the guilt was great. The Church was in the midst of a great healing revival. As many as five thousand were added to the Church in one day. Mighty miracles were taking place, "And with great power gave the apostles witness of the resurrection of the Lord Jesus." (Acts 4:33). Many signs and wonders were accomplished by the hands of the apostles, insomuch that they brought in the sick from the cities around Jerusalem, and they were healed every one. (Acts 5:12, 15, 16). Ananias and Sapphira were attracted by the power of the revival, but their interest was purely a selfish one, and it meant nothing to them except what they could profit from it in some material way. They sold certain of their property, and to make an impression upon the apostles and, perhaps to gain prestige and prominence, they told Peter that they were giving the Church all the money they had received from it. For this shameless duplicity in the midst of a great moving of God, they were visited with Divine judgment. In this case it was more than a matter of sickness; both were struck down by sudden death. This incident is not the only one of its kind that has happened in the history of the Church. Would it have done any good to have prayed for them? John says, "There is a sin unto death," and for such cases prayer will not avail.

When Paul and Barnabas were evangelizing in Cyprus, one Bar-jesus, who claimed to be a prophet, met the apostles, and sought to withstand them. He used all his wiles to prevent the governor of the land, who showed a disposition to listen to the Gospel, from being influenced by the apostle's message. It appeared as if the sorcerer might be successful in hindering the revival. The false prophet, however, reckoned wrongly. Paul, filled with the Holy Ghost, turned to him and announced that blindness was to come upon him for his wickedness in hindering men from receiving the gospel. So it happened, and he was forced to get someone to lead him about by the hand. This ended the opposition, and the governor, astonished at this manifestation of Divine power, believed upon and accepted Christ. (Acts 13:6-12). There is no doubt that many have been stricken down by a curse simply because of personal jealousy or for other reasons that they have opposed the work of God.

There is also the example of the professing Christian in the Corinthian church upon whom judgment came because of an exceptionally wicked act. The man had committed the crime of incest, the taking of his father's wife. Paul dealt with the case, not by ecclesiastical means, but by pronouncing judgment upon the man:

"For I verily, as absent in body, but present in spirit, have judged already, as though I were present, concerning him that hath so done this deed. In the name of our Lord Jesus Christ, when ye are gathered together, and my spirit, with the power of our Lord Jesus Christ. To deliver such an one unto Satan for the destruction of the flesh, that the spirit may be saved in the day of the Lord Jesus." (I Cor. 5:3-5).

The incestuous church member had brought sin into the assembly, and so was turned over to "Satan for the destruction of the flesh, that the spirit may be saved in the day of the Lord Jesus Christ." (I Cor. 5:5). No doubt this man, after the judgment of God came upon him, had sought deliverance. No one likes to be ill, not even the devil. But immediate relief was not available. He had offended God and the Church of Christ. The man had to be taught a lesson. He was turned over to the devil — cut off from the Body of Christ — and fortunately the man did learn his lesson. After much suffering, he at length came to the place where he was sorrowful for his sins. Paul in writing his second letter to the Corinthians, advised that since the man had learned his lesson, they should forgive the man. We may understand that with the forgiveness of his sin, he was restored physically. (II Cor. 2:6-8).

We have seen similar instances as this take place, and how God has suddenly taken the most rebellious and stiffnecked individual and withdrawn His protection from him, allowing the devil to visit him with affliction. We have seen God raise such persons up again, but not until they had thoroughly repented of their insubordination and wickedness. In such case, it is useless for the sick person to seek relief until he has thoroughly repented of his sin against God and the Church.

Nor were the foregoing instances the only recorded similar cases in the ministry of Paul. There were the cases of Hymenaeus and Alexander, whom the apostle turned over to Satan that they might be taught not to blaspheme. (I Tim.

1:19-20). It seems that these men, anxious to draw disciples after them, introduced certain false doctrines into the Church, even teaching that the resurrection was already past. (II Tim. 2:17, 18). Such a false teaching fundamentally is a grave sin against the Body of Christ, for it denies the glorification that awaits it at the coming of Christ. Only those who have a twisted or perverted idea of the Gospel could tolerate, let alone advocate, a teaching that denies the resurrection. This heresy was so serious that Paul was justified in invoking judgment upon these false teachers. Such men could not expect healing until they had repented of their error.

Chapter X

Satan's Desire for a Body

"Now the body is . . . for the Lord; and the Lord for the body. Know ye not that your bodies are members of Christ? What? Know ye not that your body is the temple of the Holy Ghost which is in you, which ye have of God, and ye are not your own?" (I Cor. 6:13, 15, 19).

PAUL in First Corinthians, tells us much about this Body of the Lord. In the verses above, we see that God's great plan for His people is that they might be a habitation, or a temple for the Spirit of God to dwell within. That is the great purpose for which man has been brought into this world—that God might dwell within him and manifest His life through him. Therefore God has ordained that as we partake of Christ, we become one Bread and one Body in Him. (I Cor. 10:17).

From this it can be seen how tremendously important it is that we yield our bodies as a dwelling place to the Holy Spirit. Man is not complete in himself, but has been so created that he can never be satisfied until Christ dwells within him.

It is at this point that we are confronted with a solemn fact. Satan is also a spirit and he also desires a body. When we speak of Satan, we of course also include the multitude of demon spirits that operate under his dominion. These evil spirits are at liberty and constantly wander about over the earth's surface looking for a body to inhabit. They cannot, however, enter a body at will, but there must be certain favorable circumstances existing after which they can enter and take control. Let us turn to the Eleventh Chapter of Luke, and learn from the words of Jesus some remarkable facts about this matter.

In this chapter we read the account of the Lord's healing of a dumb man, by casting out a devil. The jealous Pharisees charged Him with casting out devils through Beelzebub, the chief of devils. The Lord answers this blasphemy, however, by declaring that if Satan cast out Satan, his kingdom will not stand. He adds that He, Jesus, accomplishes this work through "the finger of God." (Luke 11:14-23). The Lord also solemnly warns the caviling Jews of the danger of committing the unpardonable sin, for which there is no forgiveness. Despite this warning, there are those today who commit this sin with utter disregard of the fearful consequences.

Then the Lord gave a warning to the man that was healed, as well as to the others present in the following words:

"When the unclean spirit is gone out of a man, he walketh through dry places, seeking rest; and finding none, he saith, I will return unto my house whence I came out. And when he cometh, he findeth it swept and garnished. Then goeth he, and taketh to him seven other spirits more wicked than himself; and they enter in, and dwell there; and the last state of that man is worse than the first." (Luke 11:24-26).

Now notice the significance of this warning. Sometimes a man's illness is caused by demon possession. At other times it is merely enemy oppression, as distinguished in Acts 10:38: "How God anointed Jesus of Nazareth with the Holy Ghost and with power; who went about doing good, and healing all that were *oppressed of the devil;* for God was with him." However, the worst form of these oppressions— demon possession—is mentioned in the case of the healing of this dumb man..Jesus related how an ejected demon walks through dry places seeking rest, but finding none. The evil spirit desires a body to clothe itself; yet he cannot at will enter any person unless the hedge of protection God has ordained, is broken down. (Job 1:10). The physical body as God has created it, naturally resists an intruding spirit. Failing to find another body in which he can easily enter, the demon bethinks himself of the house from whence he was cast out. He returns and is gratified to find it "swept and garnished." He loses no time. He goes and gathers to him seven other spirits more wicked than himself and they enter the man, and the last state is worse than the first.

Now in this tragic story there is a tremendous lesson regarding some who have been delivered by the power of God, have made professions of faith and then later become repossessed by the power of the devil. What has happened that has brought about this sad result? Notice: nothing is said about the man's going into deep sin, nor committing any great crime. Nevertheless, he has made a tragic mistake for which he is doubly guilty.

No human being is complete in himself. Man was created to be a temple of the Holy Spirit. In this case an evil spirit had gotten possession of the man, but Christ cast out the demon and he was gloriously delivered. But what happened? Is the man grateful? Does he now respond by inviting Christ to dwell within his life—for the Lord only comes by invitation; it is the devil who forces his way. There is a spiritual vacuum within the soul of every man, that is certain to be filled sooner or later. The evil spirit that once dwelt within him is walking through dry places, and will return ere long. How important that the man occupy his life with spiritual things, that he will partake of the bread of Christ, that his body may become a temple of the Holy Ghost. Once he has done that, when and if the demon returns, there will be no place for him.

Alas, some foolishly continue on in their old way. They fail to attend the house of God. They take little or no time to pray. They do not partake of the Word of God, which is the Bread of Life. They do not understand that man shall not live by (natural) bread alone, but by every word that proceedeth from the mouth of God. They ignore instruction of those who would help them and are content to go their own way. The devil at last returns with seven other devils, and the victims are in a worse state than they were before.

Notice, the man Jesus spoke of was not charged with wrong doing or of some dastardly crime. His great sin was violation of the first commandment: to love the Lord with all his heart and strength and mind. But although he has had a mighty experience of God's power to deliver, and has been set free, yet he is ungrateful and neglects to ask Christ to have pre-eminence in his life.

In other words, he does not discern the Lord's Body. His body was a temple of the Holy Ghost. But instead of inviting the Holy Ghost to take possession of his life, his "house" is "swept and garnished," unwittingly set in order for some other inhabitant rather than the Holy Spirit. Soon the man is back in the toils of Satan again.

One of the outstanding Scriptural illustrations of the above truth is found in the life of Saul. Samuel had said to Saul in his happier days that, "the Spirit of the Lord will come upon thee, and thou shalt prophesy with them and be turned into another man." The early days of Saul began auspiciously and were full of promise. But the time came when Saul became disobedient and was given to jealousy. Although warned, he paid no attention, and continued in a self-willed course. Eventually "the Spirit of the Lord departed from Saul, and an evil spirit from the Lord troubled him." (I Sam. 16:14). For a time God was merciful to the wayward king, and when David the sweet singer of

Israel ministered to him, playing on his harp, the evil spirit left Saul and the sickness of his mind left him. "And it came to pass, when the evil spirit from God was upon Saul, that David took an harp, and played with his hand: so Saul was refreshed, *and was well*, and the evil spirit departed from him." Nevertheless the king persisted in his rash conduct, and the evil spirit returned. This time his abode became permanent.

There was also the case of Abimelech, a wicked usurper in the days of the Judges, who slew seventy of his brethren. He so far forgot the example of his father Gideon, that in his desire for power he murdered his own brethren. Because of this treachery, God permitted an evil spirit to come upon him. (Judges 9:23).

Perhaps the most tragic result of a demon that takes control of a man's life is that the individual does not seem to know that he has departed from God. Not until the day before he died, did Saul seem to realize that God had departed from him. (I Sam. 28:6). This was also the case with Samson, who because of his carnal conduct, forfeited the presence of God. "He wist not that the Lord was departed from him." (Judge 16:20).

REMEMBER: *When one is healed, it is all-important that he begin serving the Lord with all his heart. The Lord will not enter without invitation. If one does not let his life be filled with the Spirit of Christ, the enemy will then come in without invitation, and the last state will be worse than the first.*

Chapter XI

Care of the Body---Eating "Worthily"

"For he that eateth and drinketh unworthily, eateth and drinketh damnation to himself, not discerning the Lord's body." (I Cor. 11:29).

IT IS evident that the above Scripture refers primarily to the partaking of the Lord's Supper. Yet the context shows that it has a wider significance than that. Paul tells us while on this same subject that "Whether therefore ye eat, or drink, or whatsoever ye do, do all to the glory of God." (I Cor. 10:31). In the seventh verse he warned "Neither be ye idolaters, as were some of them: as it is written, The people sat down to eat and drink, and rose up to play." Food and play can become idols. In Romans 14, the apostle gives further instructions on eating. In verse six, he declares that "He that eateth, eateth to the Lord, for he giveth God thanks." In the 20th verse he adds that "it is evil for that man who eateth with offence."

The Apostle Paul preludes his instructions on the Lord's Supper with the remark that many of the Corinthian Christians were not eating in a way that was pleasing to God. He said, "For in eating every one taketh before other his own supper: and one is hungry and another is drunken." (I Cor. 11:21). In other words these people were food drunkards, and their eating habits had so enslaved them that they regularly brought large supplies of food to church for gluttonous repasts under the guise of eating the Lord's Supper. He rebukes them sharply for this, and tells them that they are eating and drinking unworthily, and as a result perhaps reaping sickness and affliction. He goes on to tell them that their eating, whether at home or at the Lord's Table, was to be done circumspectly, with moderation, and "discerning the Lord's body."

Going back to the Lord's dealings with the Church in the wilderness, it will be recalled that immediately after the redemption of the Children of Israel, God gave them the Covenant of healing. No sooner had He done this than He gave instructions in two matters which are deeply significant because of the time they were given—that is immediately after the Covenant of healing. Here God delivered to the people, instruction concerning certain health habits. There are certain laws of the body which must be obeyed if the people of God are to maintain this health that God had promised them. One is in the matter of diet. The other is regarding the rest that should be given the body.

It is evident that unless people observe the laws which God has established concerning proper eating and normal resting of the body, they may get sick. Proper care of the body is closely associated with health. Many Christians seem to be unaware of this fact, and suppose that regardless of what they do in this respect, the fact that a minister prays for them should mean that they should be healed. Failing to get their healing, many, instead of seeking the cause of their sickness, are content to believe that healing is not for them, supposing that the fault lies elsewhere than in themselves.

When the Children of Israel entered the wilderness, they came into a region where there was no food. God graciously gave them manna from heaven, which we may be sure contained all the elements of a balanced diet. It was pleasant tasting, like unto wafers and honey. (Ex. 16:31). On occasions, the Lord sent a wind which also brought up quails, providing a variation in their diet. (Vs. 13). This provision however did not satisfy all of the people. The mixed multitude, which included many non-Israelites, fell to lusting and wanted *flesh* all the time. (Num. 11:4-6). Notice God's attitude in the matter. He acceded to their request and sent them quails. But the Psalmist commenting on the incident says: "(They) lusted exceedingly in the wilderness, and tempted God in the desert. And he gave them their request; but sent leanness into their soul." (Psa. 106: 14, 15). Until this time there had been no feeble ones among their tribes, but now a plague struck the camp, which fell particularly upon the people that had lusted. (Num. 11:33, 34). The account states that the plague was very great and many died as a result of it.

Notice in the context, the Apostle's reference to this event when he said, "Neither let us tempt Christ, as some of them tempted, and were destroyed of serpents." (I Cor. 10:9-10). What was this sin that the Children of Israel committed that caused sickness and death to come into their midst? *It was the sin of complaining about the food that the Lord had given them.* They said, "Our soul loatheth this light bread." (Num. 21:5). They were not satisfied with the diet which the Lord had given them and which had brought perfect health to the people. Then came the fiery serpents which bit many, resulting in their death. It was then that the Lord gave instructions to Moses to put up a Brazen Serpent on a pole, and whosoever looked upon the Brass Serpent was healed. *Notice that God did not send the remedy until the Children of Israel repented of their sin.* After they had sought God's forgiveness, then Moses prayed for them, and deliverance came by the Brass Serpent which Jesus said was a type of Him. (John 3:14). God is gracious, kind and forgiving, but He expects us to obey His laws. Thus we see that with the promise of healing given to God's people, the Scriptures immediately follow with a lesson on the manner of their diet. Since these things were written for our instruc-

Care of the Body—Eating "Worthily" 63

tion, it is impossible to understand the matter otherwise than that God is calling attention to the truth that His people should live on a simple diet and avoid lusting for rich foods. That while certain foods might be permissible on occasion, the regular demand for a rich diet is not conducive to health. We are to eat to live, not to live to eat. It is to be observed that the promise of health in Exodus 15:26 is subject to obedience to God's commandments.

The same great lesson is taught in the Book of Daniel. The prophet and his companions had been taken to Babylon. The king appointed to them the rich diet of the court, which consisted of wines and rich meats. But Daniel purposed in his heart that he would not defile himself with the king's meat, and made a request for a more simple diet of pulse, or vegetables. The king's servant was reluctant to heed this request, but after a test period of ten days, it was found that the countenances of Daniel and his friends were fairer than those who partook of the king's meat. Is it not clear that Divine inspiration in permitting this incident to be recorded is seeking to teach men the laws of health? It is significant that Daniel lived through the long 70-year captivity, an intensely active life and was still sound in mind and body three years after the Children of Israel had returned back to their land at the appointment of Cyrus the King. (Dan. 10:1). That shows Daniel must have been nearly a hundred years of age.

The chief danger of over-eating is that when more food is taken into the body than is necessary to supply the body with nourishment, the excess food turns into fat. The truth is that excess fat is the greatest killer of all. It has been said that aged people are rarely troubled from obesity, because extremely fat people usually never live to be old. This is a common fact. Any physician or insurance actuary will tell you that at the age of 60, five fat men will die before one man who is normal in weight. This is a serious matter. An insurance man considers an overweight person at middle age an extremely poor risk, and usually will not sell him life insurance unless he brings his weight down.

Why is fat the killer? Simply because it adds a great number of extra blood vessels through which blood must be pumped. In order to accomplish this added task, the heart must pump much harder. Therefore it wears out sooner, breaks down on the job, and the victim dies. Heart trouble is the great killer and the cause of it in most cases is excess fat caused by either excessive eating or an unbalanced diet. Other diseases, such as diabetes, liver trouble, and many other complaints are caused by overweight.

Usually people in this condition seek an easy way out of their difficulties. They want God to heal them. Well and good. But how can they maintain their healing unless they begin to obey the laws of health which God has ordained? This writer well remembers a patient afflicted with serious trouble in her limbs, so that she had to have the support of crutches in order to walk. Had God instantly healed her she would not have been able to walk—she was so much overweight. Such individuals may be said to be literally digging their graves with their teeth.

On another occasion a young lady gave us a request for prayer. Like most young ladies of marriageable age, she desired to maintain a school-girl figure. Being overweight she remarked that she desired prayer so that she would lose weight. We looked at her solemnly and quoted, "This kind cometh not out, but by prayer and fasting." Perhaps the answer sounded frivolous, but actually we were speaking seriously. There is no way to reduce the deadly overweight except to follow a proper diet, or by fasting, which latter method few people are willing to follow. Perhaps here we should make a few remarks about fasting.

Care of the Body—Eating "Worthily"

Many people groan at the word "fasting," and say that they cannot fast. Yet all of us should have occasional seasons of fasting. We do not refer at this time to long fasts, which no doubt are not for everyone. However, special blessing is promised by the Lord Jesus to attend fasting, and indeed it is sad that in view of the alarming spiritual state of our nation at the present time, that the whole Church is not upon her knees in prayer and fasting.

Nevertheless, we do not speak of fasting as a means of reducing. Fasting is indeed a method of reducing, but it is not the most efficient method. Actually one may eat and reduce. Informed people know that proper reducing diets which contain a preponderance of fruits and vegetables, with an absence of breads, and fats, actually cause the person to lose weight faster than if he ate no food at all! Thus has God through nature generously provided the means by which any person may get rid of unnecessary weight, which if he continues to carry will result in his signing his own death warrant, whereas otherwise he might have had many additional years. Books describing the proper diet for reducing without fasting may be obtained for a reasonable sum at any bookstore.

If heart trouble were the only consequence of overweight, it would be bad enough, but unbalanced diets result in diabetes, cataracts, kidney trouble, and a whole host of ailments. For most people, even after they have been healed, permanent health cannot be assured unless that person, like Daniel of old, is willing to follow the laws of health intelligently and to avoid rich foods which cause overweight with its long list of attendant woes. Just as Christians must obey the laws of God if they are to maintain a healthy spiritual experience, so they must obey the laws of health. God has ordained that those who would have health may not disregard its laws with impunity.

CHAPTER XII

Care of the Body---Rest

THE second notable fact which follows the promise of Divine healing in Exod. 15:26, is the commandment that the people of God should take one day in seven for rest. Why did God give this commandment? Obviously the primary reason was that the human body needs one day in seven for rest. On that day the Children of Israel were not to go about their ordinary employment, but after six days they were to forego their labors and observe a day of rest. This was not an arbitrary rule. As a matter of fact, the human body is so constituted that it needs this periodic change. Unless it gets it, poisons in the system build up, resistance is lowered, and disease may get a foothold. It is a common fact that the reason many people are ill is simply because they have failed to take proper care of their bodies. The body is a member of the Body of Christ, and Christians are responsible for its proper care.

A man came to us in a meeting some time ago, declaring he was in serious physical condition and desired immediate prayer. We told him that as there were thousands waiting to be prayed for he must await his turn. In the meantime we advised him to attend the services, that his faith might be strengthened. He replied that he worked each night of the week and was unable to come. He was asked to come Sunday, but he replied that he regularly worked that day also. Our answer to him was that since he insisted on breaking the

Care of the Body—Rest

law of God by working every day of the week, we could not pray for his healing until he ceased this violation of the law of health.

Ministers and their wives are often guilty of this transgression of the laws of health. Sunday is usually for them an exacting day. When Monday comes, often they feel that burdens of the pastorate are pressing and consequently they take no time for rest. Sooner or later they crack up. Many pastors' wives are in a serious physical condition for no other reason than this. Is Divine healing what they need?

Perhaps. God is gracious, and often has more compassion on us than we deserve. Yet if we go on breaking the laws of health, in the end we must pay for the violation. When the body gets in a run-down condition there is usually only one remedy, and that is rest. The length of this rest will depend more or less on the length of time that the body's physical resources have been squandered. Yet countless people who have thus abused their bodies get in the healing line, and when they fail to get deliverance, suppose that Divine healing doesn't work for them. It usually doesn't occur to them to seek the cause of their trouble.

Some Christian workers harm their bodies by their failure to take proper care of them under the mistaken impression that the time to work for the Lord, being so short, they dare not take any time for rest. Yet we find that Jesus, Whose days of earthly ministry were so very few, and though the salvation of the world depended upon Him, not only took time for rest but commanded His disciples to do likewise. After sending the Twelve out on a preaching and Divine healing mission (Mark 6:7-13),the apostles returned telling about the wonderful things that had taken place. Christ might have replied, that the harvest being so plenteous and the laborers so few, the disciples should immediately return to the work. But no! In Mark 6:31 it is recorded that the Lord said, "Come ye yourselves apart into a desert place, and rest awhile." Was the time lost? No! Refreshed, the apostolic party returned to the field and healing virtue was present in the next service in such a degree that "as many as touched him were made whole." (Mark 6:56).

Perhaps the most impressive example of how failure to care for the body may result in serious illness, is found in the 2nd chapter of Philippians. Here we are informed of the case of Ephaphroditus. He was commended by Paul as a most faithful laborer, yet he was sick, and so seriously so, that for a time Paul despaired of his life. Why was this? We are informed that it was because he had gone beyond his strength in the greatest of all causes — the cause of the Gospel. It seems that the Apostle Paul was laboring at Philippi and he had not been properly taken care of by the members of the church. It was a new assembly and the congregation, it seemed, was not as diligent in their care of the apostle as they might have been. When Paul first went to Philippi he had been beaten and imprisoned, though afterwards released through the result of an earthquake of supernatural origin. Now he was in prison again. (Phil. 1:13). Having so suffered for the church at Philippi, the members might have seen that the apostle's wants were properly supplied while he was in prison. Apparently they failed in this. Ephaphroditus took this burden upon himself. In so doing this, he went beyond his strength and as a result, his body was struck down with a sickness that nearly took his life. As Paul says, "Because for the work of Christ he was nigh unto death, not regarding his life, to supply your lack of service toward me." (Phil. 2:30).

Although Epaphroditus was engaged in a most worthy cause — the care of a neglected apostle, who was chained in a prison — yet nevertheless, he suffered physically. What then shall we say of those who fail to take care of their bodies for less worthy causes? Notice also, that Epaphroditus' restora-

Care of the Body—Rest

tion was not instantaneous. God had mercy on him, but the context implies that he slowly convalesced. Why? Because it takes time for the body to recuperate after its nervous energy has been depleted. All things are possible with God, but usually in the case where the body is ill because of the lack of proper rest, time is needed before a complete restoration takes place.

It may be asked, why is it that a person who overstrains his body should become ill? The answer is, that about us on every hand are the germs of deadly disease. Usually they cause no harm because the natural defensive agencies of the body destroy them. But once the human constitution gets into a run-down condition, these defensive agencies are unable to function effectively. Disease germs and bacteria rapidly multiply and gain ascendancy. On the other hand, when the body is rested, the full strength of its natural forces is able to resist and destroy that which seeks its harm.

There is much more that might be added on matters related to what we have been discussing. Summed up, the facts are that we should use discretion in the care of the body, just as we would in the operation of a fine automobile. There are circumstances and conditions under which a car should not be driven. Likewise we should not push ourselves beyond our strength and ability. He who drives himself unreasonably may finally wind up in a state of nervous exhaustion. We should use common sense in the activities of daily life. An individual who goes in swimming when the air is cold may suffer from exposure. A person who sits in a draft may catch a cold. There is need of the use of common sense in all these things. We should not expect to enjoy continuous health unless we are wise in our conduct in these matters.

CHAPTER XIII

The Body Is the Temple of the Lord

"Know ye not that your bodies are the members of Christ? Shall I then take the members of Christ, and make them the members of an harlot? God forbid. What? Know ye not that your body is the temple of the Holy Ghost, which is in you, and ye have of God, and ye are not your own? For ye are bought with a price; therefore, glorify God in your body, and in your spirit, which are God's." (I Cor. 6:15, 20.)

BECAUSE the believer, upon receiving the Spirit of Christ, becomes a member of the Lord's Body, he becomes actually the temple of the Holy Ghost. This is an awesome fact. Consider that the Holy Spirit once dwelt within the Holy of Holies behind the inner veil of the temple, where only the High Priest dared enter once a year, and then with blood. But now the Lord has withdrawn from temples of stone and has made His dwelling elsewhere. Where? Amazing thing! He has chosen to dwell within the temple or body of the believer! This being true, how then ought the believer to walk?

There had been fornication in the Corinthian Church. Paul in writing to the church, shrinks back in horror at the thought. What! Take the members of Christ and make them the members of an harlot! God forbid! The body is the temple of the Holy Ghost and is therefore holy. The believer should keep from the very appearance of evil, let alone to indulge in gross sin.

When the gift of discernment is manifest in the ministry of prayer for the sick, some very significant things have been observed. Individuals who have been unfaithful in their marriage life and have not repented, but who nevertheless seek healing, have been sternly rebuked by the Spirit of God. People cannot trifle with God in matters like this. Violation of the laws of purity strikes a blow at the very heart of Christianity. It cannot be tolerated. Only deep repentance and the individual's acceptance of the blood of Jesus Christ as a covering may suffice to cleanse away the gravity of such a crime. Yet there are such people who time and again get in the healing line and seek deliverance. They should repent first of their deeds before they may look for healing. The apostle says we dare not take the members of Christ and make them the members of an harlot. Those who do and yet profess Christ are partaking of Christ unworthily and in so doing they are receiving a curse rather than a blessing. "For he that eateth and drinketh unworthily, eateth and drinketh damnation to himself, not discerning the Lord's body. For this cause many are weak and sickly..."

It is interesting to note that there is another thing the Spirit of God often draws to attention during prayer for the sick. The use of tobacco is sharply rebuked. Why is God so opposed to a believer's using tobacco? Because the body is the temple of the Holy Ghost. God does not want to dwell within a body profaned by this unclean habit.

What is wrong with tobacco? It contains no less than nineteen poisons, of which nicotine is only one. Nicotine raises the blood pressure and gives the person a momentary feeling of a "lift". Reaction, however, soon sets in and the smoker quickly feels the necessity of another "lift". These combinations of poisons have the peculiar effect, common to drugs, of exciting the nervous system and giving it the momentary pleasurable reaction which, however, in a few minutes is followed by a depression, and makes the smoker desire another cigarette. This cycle goes on indefinitely.

Saltpetre has been added to the cigarette paper to assist in keeping the cigarette burning. Discarded cigarettes often smoulder on to cause millions of dollars worth of damage, although this is one of the very least of tobacco's evil results.

The tobacco smoker soon becomes indifferent to the rights of others. In a closed room his cigar or pipe causes an odor that is extremely offensive to non-smokers. The smoker ignores this, however. His tobacco craving is so strong that thought of the rights of others is completely crowded out. While traveling on trains we have noted that there is not an hour of the night that some smoker is not awake, polluting the atmosphere with cigarette or cigar smoke.

Some have tried to condone their use of tobacco by pointing to what they call the habit of coffee drinking. We hold no brief for coffee drinkers but the comparison is far-fetched. If drinking coffee produces a habit, it should be broken off as any other habit. However, to compare the drinking of coffee to the habit of smoking is utterly unintelligent. A smoker dare not leave his house without a supply of cigarettes, and during the day he may smoke anywhere from twenty to forty cigarettes. Imagine a person habitually going about with twenty cups of coffee to drink!

What an indignity to the temple of the Holy Ghost is the exhalation of a cloud of tobacco smoke from the lungs. Smoking is a lust that has a kindred affinity to other physical lusts of the body. The use of tobacco is the mark of a non-Christian, although alas, there are not a few professed Christians who are slaves to its power.

What is wrong with tobacco? It defiles the temple of God, and he that defileth the temple of God, "him shall God destroy." (I Cor. 3:17.) Certainly the Lord Jesus Who is our example, would not smoke a cigarette. Yet the believer's body is a member of the Body of Christ. The Christian's use of tobacco introduces, as it were, this filthy poison into the body of Christ. Is it any wonder that some users of nicotine, who profess to be followers of Christ, are afflicted in body, and

The Body Is the Temple of the Lord 73

cannot get healed? For shame! Let him that professes the name of Christ turn from this abomination.

No one who uses tobacco and claims to be a Christian can do so without injuring his influence. Some say they feel no compunction of conscience about the matter. The Scripture (I Cor. 8:9-13), however, warns us that we are not to allow our liberty (or in this case is it license?) to become a stumbling block to others. "Wherefore, if meat make thy brother to offend, I will eat no flesh while the world standeth, lest I make my brother to offend." How many have lost confidence in the church when they found some teacher or deacon indulging in the habit of smoking?

Due to the enormous profits from the tobacco business, doctors and physicians of unethical character have been bribed to make statements deprecating the harmfulness that the tobacco habit causes. Most secular magazines which receive much of their revenue from tobacco advertisements, dare not publish the actual truth concerning this menace to health. However, the Reader's Digest which takes no advertising, and is therefore not under pressure from this source, has declared the facts about this matter repeatedly. In the December, 1952, issue of this magazine in an article entitled CANCER BY THE CARTON, the following remarks are made concerning the harmfulness of tobacco:

"During the period 1920 to 1948, deaths from (lung cancer) increased more than ten times.... At the present time cancer of the mouth and respiratory tract kills 19,000 men and 5,000 women annually in the United States.... It is frightening to speculate on the possible number of cigarettes consumed in the two decades from 1930 to 1950 ... the risk of developing the disease increases in simple proportion with the amount smoked, and may be 50 times as great among those who smoked 25 or more cigarettes daily as among nonsmokers." This then is the conclusion of medical research as recorded in the READER'S DIGEST.

Cancer is only one of the evil results of the use of tobacco. Its harm reaches out in a multitude of ways. How futile to seek healing, as long as one is committed to offering up burnt-offerings to the nicotine god. What has been said about tobacco also is true in the matter of the use of alcoholic beverages. The curse attached to those who are habituated to the consumption of strong drink is so obvious, that there would be little profit in contending with any who would be inclined to dispute this fact. One could exercise little faith for the healing of a person who in the slightest degree justified the use of these poisons, so thoroughly condemned by the scriptures.

Tobacco is altogether an evil habit. It is one that becomes so strong that in many cases it cannot be broken by human strength. The user who begins the habit so lightly in most cases smokes on to his grave. He becomes a slave to it. Though he may not have money to buy bread, yet he will find the wherewithal to get cigarettes. Beggars on the street, who claim to be in dire circumstance, often have tobacco on their breath. Like the thirst for alcoholic liquor, the habit of smoking is most difficult to break. No doubt thousands have been kept out of the kingdom, because they have felt that they could not give up tobacco.

May God grant, if we profess the name of Christ and lay claim to being a Christian, and yet have defiled the temple of God by the use of any form of tobacco, that we discontinue the use of it at once, and ask God to forgive us. If we are unwilling to do that, let us not ask God for healing. For our bodies are members of the Body of Christ. Let us not introduce nicotine into that which belongs to Christ.

God will give the earnest seeker for deliverance healing from the tobacco devil or anything else. But he must come clean. He must make an earnest effort to break off this un-Christian habit. God will meet him if he will be earnest and sincere.

CHAPTER XIV

Members of One Body

NOW we have come to another important matter in connection with sickness and health in the Christian's life. We have seen that at the time of the Communion we partake of the broken body of the Lord Jesus, and that in this act we become a part of the Body of Christ. "The bread which we break, is it not the communion of the Body of Christ? For we being many are one bread and one body: for we are all partakers of that one bread." (I Cor. 10:16-17.) As a result of this wonderful work of the Spirit of God, Paul could say, "Now ye are the Body of Christ, and members in particular." (I Cor. 12:27.) Therefore, the New Testament believer enjoys the supreme privilege of being an actual member of the Body of Christ. With this wonderful privilege there is a solemn responsibility in the relationship of one member to another. They are in a real way interdependent one of the other. They are responsible for their actions one to another. When one member suffers, all suffer with it. If we injure another member we injure ourselves, because we are members of one body.

The Apostle Paul had taken note of some of the disturbances that had occurred in the Corinthian Church. The people had become divided over doctrine and some in the church were particularly contentious. (I Cor. 1:10-11.) Many of the people were carnal and there were envyings and strife among them. Paul writing to them said, "For ye are yet carnal: for whereas there is among you envying, and strife, and divisions, are ye not carnal, and walk as men?" (I Cor. 3:3). Certain individuals committed grievous sins against other Christians. (I Cor. 5:1.) Some went to law with others in the church. (I Cor. 6:1.) This division and carnality entered even into the taking of the Lord's Supper. (I Cor. 11:17-21.) Then Paul makes a statement showing that believers cannot violate the law of the Lord's Body with impunity. He declares, "For he that eateth and drinketh unworthily, eateth and drinketh damnation to himself, not discerning the Lord's body. For this cause many are weak and sickly among you, and many sleep."

Paul then shows in the 12th Chapter, beginning with the 12th verse, how that the Body is one though it has many members. "For as the body is one, and hath many members, and all the members of that one body, being many, are one body; so also is Christ."

He goes on to show that all believers are of one Spirit whether bond or free, Jew or Gentile. Nor can one member say to the other I have no need of thee. Even the more feeble members of the body are necessary. There must be no schism within the body, but all the members should have the same care one of another. Then he declares that if one member suffer the other members will suffer also. (Verses 12-26.) This last is most significant. When a member causes another member to suffer, then the offending member will suffer also. This is the law of the Body. Violation of this law may bring sickness and suffering. Nor may healing be certainly expected until the offender forsakes and repents of his sin against his brother. It is significant indeed that Paul follows up his words of admonition with his famous chapter on Divine love.

In James 5:13-16, where the command is given for the sick to call upon the elders to anoint with oil and pray for their healing, there is also a command to "Confess your faults one to another, and pray one for another, that ye may be healed." The inference is that the sickness may have been caused because of a wrong attitude toward other members of the church. "If he have committed sins, they shall be forgiven him." Forgiveness of our brethren is associated with God's forgiveness of us. The Lord's prayer that Christ taught His disciples includes the words, "forgive us our trespasses even as we forgive the trespasses of those who sin against us." In so many words the Lord said that we must forgive if we are to be forgiven: "So likewise shall my heavenly father do also unto you, if ye from your hearts forgive not every one his brother their trespasses." (Matt. 18:35.) Certainly when a Christian becomes ill, it is as necessary for him to call in any he holds a grudge against and to get the matter settled, as it is for him to ask the elders to pray for him. *Confess your faults and pray for one another that ye may be healed.* If this is not done the implication is that the person may seek healing in vain.

Jesus also added that if we learn that a brother has ought against us, we are to go to him and if possible be reconciled to him before we come to the altar and offer our gift. (Matt. 5:23-24.) What is the gift that we are to offer at the altar? Paul says, "I beseech you therefore, brethren, by the mercies of God, that ye present your bodies a living sacrifice, holy, acceptable unto God, which is your reasonable service." (Rom. 12:1.) The inference is obvious. As we present our bodies to the Holy Spirit as an acceptable sacrifice, we thus become members of the Body of Christ, and are partakers of His strength and of His health. But in so doing it is necessary for us to become reconciled to our brother. A wound and a schism in the body brings pain and suffering to all the members of the body. If we do not become reconciled one to another, then we may continue to be sick and weakly.

Recognizing the Proper Position of the Members of the Body

Not every member is given the same position in the body. "If the whole body were an eye, where were the hearing? If the whole were hearing where were the smelling? But now hath God set the members every one of them in the body, as it hath pleased him." (I Cor. 12:17-18.) Paul points out the fact that there is a tendency for the members of the Body to envy one another and to not always be satisfied with the position that God has given them. Some are not willing to submit themselves to those who are given rule over them in the Lord. He admonishes believers to "Obey them that have the rule over you and submit yourselves: for they watch for your souls, as they that must give an account, that they may do it with joy, and not with grief; for that is unprofitable for you." (Heb. 13:17.)

Alas, for those who will not obey the Divine order. Insubordination produces a wound in the Body of Christ and opens the door for sickness and disease. They do not recognize nor discern the Lord's body and therefore they suffer. Let us not be misunderstood. We do not refer to the authority of those who may hold ecclesiastical position and who actually deny the power of God. As God gives us the light we must walk in the light. We do not recommend that any Christian should continue to be a part of an organization which denies the power of God. But in those churches which are faithful to the cause of Christ, their leaders are worthy of love and confidence. For as the inspired writer has said, "They watch for your souls, as they that must give an account."

There was the case of Miriam and Aaron who spoke against the authority of Moses: "Hath the Lord indeed spoken only by Moses? hath he not spoken also by us? And the Lord heard it." (Num. 12:3.) The story is familiar to all Bible readers. The Lord said that He had given Moses a special position as leader of the congregation of Israel.

"Wherefore then were ye not afraid to speak against my servant Moses?" (Vs. 8.) And when the Cloud departed from off the tabernacle they looked and lo Miriam had become leprous. Miriam was healed in answer to the supplication of Moses who prayed, "Heal her now, O God, I beseech thee." (Vs. 13.) She was healed, but not before there was repentance. Even then seven days were required before the healing was manifest so that she could be permitted to return to the camp. (Vss. 14-15.) The lesson is clear. Insubordination to God-ordained authority may result in sickness and disease as was the case of Miriam. God hath set members in the Body as it hath pleased Him, and the rest of us are required to cooperate and respect God's appointments. More than one sick person in a congregation may trace his illness to rebellion against God's shepherd.

The same sin of rebellion, in a more intensified degree, was committed by the company of Korah. Their action became an open rebellion. As a result of their treachery, the earth opened her mouth and they were carried down alive into the pit. (Num. 16:32-34.) When the Children of Israel joined in the spirit of the rebellion, a plague broke out and only the intercession of Moses and Aaron stayed the plague. Aaron took incense and made an atonement for the people. "And he stood between the dead and the living; and the plague was stayed." (Num. 16:47-48.)

To these instances we could add the case of Uzziah the king. He thought to usurp the ministry of the priests, but leprosy smote him, from which he did not recover to the day of his death. Uzziah had been a good king, and had served the Lord well for many years. But alas, in II Chron. 26:16, we are told, "But when he was strong, his heart was lifted up to his destruction; for he transgressed against the Lord his God, and went into the temple to burn incense upon the altar of incense." It is evident from these things that it is necessary for the believer to recognize his place and the place of others in the Body of Christ. He must labor not just for his own good, but for the good of the whole Body. If he does not, he is sinning against the Body, and as a result he may become weak and sickly, not discerning the Lord's Body. If we are sick, and we find that we have ought in our heart against our brother, or if we have been contentious or of a rebellious spirit, then let us repent, and make the restitution that is necessary. We may then have definite reason to expect to share in the health of the Body of Christ.

Discerning the Whole Body of Christ

So far, we have considered the believer's place in the Body of Christ as he is related to other believers in the local assembly. There is another phase that is still less understood, but which is just as important. The Body of Christ includes more than just local believers, or those in a certain organization, but indeed must include believers everywhere. "For by one Spirit are we all baptised into one body, whether we be Jews or Gentiles, whether we be bond or free; and have been all made to drink into one Spirit." (I Cor. 12:13.) From this verse we see that we must not only recognize the members of our local church, but we must recognize the relationship of all the members that are a part of the Body.

In our book "World Evangelization Now", we wrote: "The Church's failure to recognize all the members of its body has resulted in sickness in its members. For example, one of the members that God has set in the Church is gifts of healing. (I Cor. 12:28.) There are those who profess to be of the Body who oppose such gifts. Some nominally accept Divine healing, but look with disfavor upon, or are unduly critical of those who have the gifts in operation in their ministries. Such persons or groups, by their attitude, fail to discern the members that God has set in his Body, and therefore fail to discern the Body of Christ. They thus cut themselves off from a normal functioning of the Body. A man can live without arms or legs or ears, but he cannot live normally. People who insist in identifying themselves with those who refuse to recognize these members of the Body of Christ, can hardly expect to receive or enjoy the blessings of healing in that atmosphere of doubt and skepticism.

"The Church may only have the health that it should, when all of its members are recognized and permitted to normally function in their midst. Sectarianism has hampered the Church from the days of Jesus until the present day. The apostles, when they saw one casting out devils in the Name of Jesus, but who did not have apostolic credentials, sought to forbid the man from ministering. Jesus rebuked that attitude and told them, "Forbid him not." (Luke 9:50.) Such a sectarian spirit was manifested on more than one occasion in the days of the Early Church. At one time certain brethren attempted to divide the Church on the matter of circumcision. (Acts 15). At another time a strong division appeared in the Corinthian Church over the matter of water-baptism; one group followed after Paul, another after Apollos, and another after Peter. (I Cor. 1:11-13.) To avoid such divisions, Paul ceased baptizing his converts and left the matter to the local churches.

"The Corinthians were not discerning the unity of the Body of Christ. Therefore as a result, many were weak and sickly. Where there is division there is all manner of evil. Envy, strife, division, and sectarian pride, cause men to build a fence of exclusion about themselves. Organizations are working agreements between believers, and working agreements are necessary but they are not to be confounded with the Body of Christ. True believers in any group are indeed members of the Body of Christ, yet only a part of the Body. Arguments advanced by carnal persons that any one organization comprises the entire Body of Christ, is an exceedingly grave error. Fierce debates and controversies that have raged over such things have never edified the Church but have rather served to divide and wound the Body. All men, even good men, do not simultaneously arrive at a full understanding of all phases of the truth at one time. This always has been true. "Now we see through a glass, darkly; but then face to face." "Knowledge puffeth up, but (love) edifieth." If we are to see the Church healed spiritually and physically, then we must recognize the whole Body, even though its members are still imperfect in knowledge. There is a line to be drawn, of course, but the line of demarcation is plain. It is impossible to have true fellowship with those who deny the power of the Spirit, for it is indeed by the Spirit of God that we are baptized into one Body. That is the basis of our fellowship. Minor differences over church government, water baptism, prophetic views, and other things should not be sufficient reason for dividing the Body of Christ. Though these matters are important, we dare not say that they are more important, or even of the same importance, as that of maintaining the unity of the Body of Christ. If we are to see the physical bodies of the individual members healed, then we must earnestly seek the spiritual healing of the entire Body."

We have not space to further elaborate on this important subject, except to add this. God has called each believer to be faithful to his own local church. But let him at all times maintain a love in his heart for other believers in Christ wherever they may be. If, however, his own church is fiercely sectarian, it is probable that he will partake of the same spirit. Such a condition may infect his soul and perhaps his health. God hasten the day when all Spirit-filled people may recognize and have fellowship one with another. So will the Church be restored to health and the wounds caused by unhappy divisions, healed.

CHAPTER XV

Paul's Thorn in the Flesh

THE apostle said that many were weak and sickly because they discern not the Body of Christ. He declared, "Now ye are the members of Christ and members in particular." We are members of the Body of Christ. We are flesh of His flesh and bone of His bone. Should the members of the Body of Christ be sick? God forbid!

There are those who seem to think that it is the will of God that the members of Christ's Body be subject to sickness. Their strongest claim to this belief seems to be Paul's "thorn in the flesh". Paul had a "thorn in the flesh" and they say that this thorn was sickness. Carrying their argument on, they point out that if so great an apostle as Paul were sick, certainly sickness must in some cases be the will of God for His people. Now if it could be proved that Paul's "thorn in the flesh" were sickness, we might concede that there were some argument in the favor of this contention. But was Paul's "thorn in the flesh" sickness? We propose to show that this assumption is entirely false and without a shred of evidence in the Scriptures.

In the first place, leading Bible expositors who are not known as exponents of the doctrine of Divine healing, admit that there is no evidence that this figure of speech relates to sickness. The Scofield Bible says about the theory of Paul's supposed sickness: "This cannot be positively known, and the reserve of the Scripture is as sure a mark of inspiration as its revelations. Paul's particular thorn is not described that his consolations may avail for all to whom any thorn is given."

Some have argued, without any proof whatever, that Paul's thorn was ophthalmia, a serious eye affliction inducing bodily weakness, and producing a condition of near-blindness. If any proof were needed that Paul was not blind, it is the fact that the Lord healed him of blindness! The Lord directed Ananias to the place where Paul was praying, that he should lay hands upon him that he might receive his sight. (Acts 9:17.) This was confirmed in a vision. (Vs. 12.) And the Scripture records that he did receive his sight. (Vs. 18.) Surely this plain statement of the Scripture should end forever further false surmises about Paul's blindness.

It is true that Paul did have "a thorn in the flesh". What was it? On this matter we ought to allow the Scriptures to explain themselves. What does the Bible say that a "thorn in the flesh" is? All agree that the term is a figure of speech and not a literal thorn. We shall see that the Scriptures use the term "thorn in the flesh" to indicate personalities and not disease. In Numbers 33:35, Moses said:

> "If ye will not drive out the inhabitants of the land from before you; then it shall come to pass that those that ye let remain of them shall be pricks in your eyes, and thorns in your sides, and shall vex you in the land wherein ye dwell."

Joshua, speaking sometime later, said, "They shall be scourges in your sides, and thorns in your eyes." (Joshua 23:13.) Again in Judges 2:3, the Lord speaks of the Canaanites as "thorns in your sides". We see, therefore, that according to the Scriptures, "a thorn in the flesh" is not a disease but a personality, whom the devil uses to annoy, to persecute or trouble the children of God.

Paul's "thorn in the flesh" must have been something similar. Many times the apostle had triumphed over his opposers. On one occasion a man who would hinder him was stricken with blindness. At another time a girl with a familiar spirit who was used of Satan to intrude upon the ministry of the apostle, was silenced when Paul with authority cast out the evil spirit. When the apostle was cast in prison, an earthquake shook the foundations and opened the doors. But there came a time when Paul no longer experienced such deliverance. Cast into prison, he languished there a long period of time, and it appeared that evil men triumphed over him. Just as the Canaanites were a "thorn in the flesh" to the Children of Israel, so these persecutors were a "thorn" to Paul. Yet there was a Divine purpose in it all. During the time Paul was imprisoned, he wrote a number of wonderful epistles. Had he been free to evangelize at that time, it is possible that they would never have been written.

There is something else for those to note who suppose Paul's "thorn in the flesh" was sickness. Just before Paul tells us about that "thorn", he lists his labours and sufferings for Christ. He said he was "in labours more abundant in stripes above measure, in prisons more frequent, in deaths oft." (II Cor. 11:23-33.) It is a long list and does not sound like the story of a sick man. If a sick person could do as much as Paul did, and suffer all those things, we might wish that kind of sickness upon all the children of God! The fact is that Paul had infirmities and sufferings, but not one place in the list is there mentioned anything about sickness. And why is the omission? Because Christians are the members of the Body of Christ. It is not the will of God that the Body of the Lord should be sick. Yea, Christ's body while on earth, suffered infirmities. It became tired and weary. Christ hungered; He thirsted. He suffered in agony for a lost world. Yea, His body died on the cross. But He was never sick. So we who are members of the Body of Christ, will suffer weariness as He suffered. We shall be subject to infirmities as He was subject. If His Coming tarries, we shall die as His body died. But since His body was never sick, then it is not the will of God that we shall become sick, for we are members of His Body. If we discern that our body is of the Body of Christ, then we shall not be weak and sickly nor die before our time.

Chapter XVI

Christ Is the Head

IN the same chapter in which we are given the revelation of the nature of the mystical Body of Christ, we have this statement in the third verse, "The head of every man is Christ." That truth is repeated in Ephesians 1:22, where it says that God gave Christ to "be the head over all things to the church." This revelation is repeated in Colossians 1:18. We are members of the Body of Christ, but it is He, Himself, Who is the Head! The guiding and ruling part of the body is the head. The members of the body are merely instruments for carrying out the will of the head. Now Christ being the Head, desires to guide the members of His Body unto the performing of His will.

Trust in the Lord

Now if Christ is the Head, and we the members of His Body, then some important things naturally follow. No longer our own, having been bought with a price, we are members of His Body to be used as He sees fit. Our life fits into a pattern that is not for our own convenience, but for the fulfillment of His great plan.

Right here is the reason for perhaps half of all the sickness in the Church of Christ. The members, instead of depending on Christ to be their Head, to direct them, to supply all their needs, to guide them in their daily lives, have to a great extent never learned to trust Christ in a practical way. They are filled with fears about the future, about circumstances, about problems in their lives, about financial needs. They do not day by day, as Daniel did, bring all their problems before the Lord, asking that His Spirit shall cause the things of their lives to flow into the Divine plan. They are moved by this thing and that thing until in many cases they get completely out of the will of God.

The Psalmist speaking in the Spirit of God, gives us the perfect answer to all this:

"This poor man cried, and the Lord heard him, and saved him out of all his troubles. The angel of the Lord encampeth round about them that fear him, and delivereth them. O taste and see that the Lord is good: blessed is the man that trusteth in him. O fear the Lord, ye his saints: for there is no want to them that fear him. The young lions do lack, and suffer hunger: but they that seek the Lord shall not want any good thing." (Psa. 34:6-10.)

"Trust in the Lord, and do good; so shalt thou dwell in the land, and verily thou shalt be fed. Delight thyself also in the Lord; and he shall give thee the desires of thine heart. Commit thy way unto the Lord; trust also in him; and he shall bring it to pass. And he shall bring forth thy righteousness as the light, and thy judgment as the noonday. Rest in the Lord, and wait patiently for him: fret not thyself because of him who prospereth in his way, because of the man who bringeth wicked devices to pass." (Psa. 37:3-7.)

"The steps of a good man are ordered by the Lord: and he delighteth in his way ... I have been young, and now am old; yet have I not seen the righteous forsaken, nor his seed begging bread.... Mark the perfect man, and behold the upright: for the end of that man is peace." (Psa. 37:23, 25, 37.)

We should read these promises again and again until they become a part of us. We are told to commit our way to the Lord. Daily, with faith and confidence, our problems should be definitely placed in the hands of God. Give God time to work. He will in season cause all things to work together for good. But here is our supreme mistake. Too many of us do not daily commit our way and our problems and our plans into the hands of God; therefore, He is forced to let us work out our own way, usually to our own loss. Failure to completely commit our way unto the Lord usually results in uncertainty, in doubts, and in fears. Fear prepares the way for the nervous conditions to which a great number of Christians are subject. Job in his affliction said, "For the thing which I greatly feared is come upon me, and that which I was afraid of is come unto me. I was not in safety, neither had I rest, neither was I quiet; yet trouble came." (Job 3:25-26.) Job had not yet learned to fully trust God. He was filled with fear and that which he feared came upon him. If Christ is our Head, we must completely trust our life to Him. Fear is the opposite of faith.

Surgeons have performed a delicate operation of the stomach which has succeeded in some cases in correcting nervous stomach disorders. The "worry nerves" are severed and they no longer carry the news of the patient's worries and anxieties to the stomach, and lo the ulcers clear up! How good it would be if we let the Great Physician sever us from our fears and worries, and that we would learn to confide and trust in Him completely. We should soon discover that our nervous conditions would clear up. In many cases that is all the person needs for complete healing. How can a person be healed of a nervous condition which is the result of worry, when he insists on continuing to worry?

What we say about the emotion of worry is true of other emotions which are uncontrolled. A fit of anger can produce symptoms of high blood pressure and other ailments. Envy, jealousy, and like emotions are destructive of health. To what purpose is prayer for people who continue to do the things that produce disease? The cause must be eliminated. Fear, envy, jealousy are diseases of the spirit. We should seek to be healed of them before the diseases of the body, which they have produced.

What is the secret of deliverance from all these things? Paul gives us the answer in Phil. 4:6:

"Be careful (anxious R. V.) for nothing; but in everything by prayer and supplication with thanksgiving let your requests be made known unto God. And the peace of God, which passeth all understanding, shall keep your hearts and minds through Jesus Christ."

This is the secret! This is the cure for nervous conditions. Daily put your problems into the hands of God. Thank Him for the answer. Let your life be fully committed to His will. Your life will become one of victory instead of defeat. Your nervous condition will be forgotten. For you are resting and trusting in the El Shaddai. With Him there is no fear, but a light that shineth unto the perfect day.

Chapter XVII

Prayer and Fasting

IT IS necessary that we steadfastly resist the devil. Satan is defeated, but he will not accept his defeat unless we resist him. "Resist the devil and he will flee from you." There is no reason why the believer should not fulfill in his life the promise of God in the matter of his health. He should prosper and be in health even as his soul prospers.

Naturally a person who is seventy years old, may not expect the same vigor as when he was twenty. It is true that a few have experienced unusual prolongation of youthful powers. Moses was such an one. (Deut. 34:7). Caleb was another. (Joshua 14:10-11). The Bible speaks of the renewing of one's youth. (Psa. 103:5). Here is a rare promise for those who may receive it. However, such a matter is not the subject for elaboration in this book. Our purpose at this present time is to lead people into an experience of dominion over sickness, that they may enjoy normal health. Not to consume it upon their pleasure, but that they might be profitable servants in the work of the kingdom of God.

There are always those who ask, "What shall we do when all else has failed?" There are some so used to defeat that their spirit has been infected with discouragement and despair, and many do not seem to be able to rid themselves of the obsession. Will fasting help such cases? Certainly we cannot rule out fasting as a means of deliverance in desperate and extreme cases. The Lord said that there were certain cases of demon possession which could not be cured without prayer and fasting. Concerning the subject of fasting let us add the following remarks, which were published some time ago in THE VOICE OF HEALING.

First of all, he who fasts must fast unto God and not unto man. Nothing could be more unwholesome or savor more of the natural man, than for a person to go about in the church and say, "I'm in the sixth day of a fast," or "I'm in the eighth day of a fast." That would be fasting unto man and not unto God. The Lord commanded that we fast in secret and our Father in heaven would reward us openly. (Matt. 6:16-18). If one obeys this, he will certainly never inject an issue into an assembly. All the benefits that might have accrued by a fast can be destroyed, if unnecessary issues are raised to engender strife and division. The damage that can be caused by fasting unto strife is clearly outlined in Isaiah 58:1-8. The benefits of a proper kind of fast are also mentioned.

Of course, there are times when the Church or a large group of people may fast as a body. (Jonah 3:7-10 and Acts 13:1-2). Obviously secrecy is not possible nor necessary then. Nor would it appear that a humble testimony from some one who had achieved a great victory in his life through fasting, be out of order.

Fasting which has the motive to make the individual a "somebody" can produce no lasting good to the person or any one else. Few will ever admit such a motive, but the heart can be deceitful. May all of us spurn self-exaltation as we would fellowship with Satan himself, who brought about his own doom from that very thing. God will use the man who will say and mean it from his heart, "He must increase, but I must decrease."

Scriptural example seems to indicate that ordinarily fasts did not extend beyond a limited time. Cornelius fasted until three o'clock in the afternoon, perhaps longer. Paul fasted three days as recorded in Acts 9:9, 19. Apparently short fasts should have a normal place in a Christian's life. (I Cor. 7:5; Mark 2:18-20).

Longer fasts on occasions are recorded in the Scriptures. These from the context, appear to have been undertaken as the result of an overwhelming need that was not answered by ordinary prayer. We must bear in mind that great crises come to at least some people which ordinary methods fail to resolve. Moses fasted forty days, at a time when it appeared that Israel was about to perish under Divine displeasure. (Exod. 32:31; 34:28). When one of the princes of Satan withstood the answer to a prayer that was divinely intended to be answered the first day, Daniel ate "no pleasant bread" for a period of three weeks. Ultimately, the answer came accompanied with the salutation from the angel, "O Daniel, a man greatly beloved." Christ began His ministry after a period in which He fasted forty days. The Scriptures state that He was "full of the Holy Ghost" before He began to fast, but after it was over He "returned in the power of the spirit." It must be noted that there appears to have been a supernatural element in some of these longest fasts for they drank no water, and no man in the natural could do this without death intervening first. (Exod. 34:28). Such fasts would not appear to be a normal pattern nor to be emulated.

A key Scripture showing the absolute necessity of fasting before certain kinds of demons can be ejected is that of Matthew 17:21. Speaking of the epileptic demon that the disciples were unable to cast out, Jesus said, "Howbeit this kind goeth not out but by prayer and fasting." All in all, the continuing of a long fast seems to be tied up in a desperate need. We can hardly avoid the fact that the need is greater now than ever before. That some should get such a burden for a world of lost men that, as Daniel of old, they should feel impelled in the Spirit to "eat no pleasant" bread for a protracted time, does not seem unreasonable.

There is another circumstance, which only one engaged in a constant ministry to the sick and suffering can fully realize, that is the extent of the crushing load of misery caused by Satanic oppression that is in the world. True, multitudes of people are finding deliverance under those who have a ministry of healing. But there are others who because of isolation, financial circumstances, or physical incapacity, cannot sit under a ministry of faith, and to them their situation appears hopeless. Is there not some tangible method that will help them to break through their weakness and unbelief—something basically simple that will help them to secure deliverance? God has been merciful to many of us, and sometimes we are prone to forget the plight of the less fortunate. Is not Matthew 17:21 the solution to these cases?

It would seem that fasts of unusual length would have significance only in connection with some desperate need. We have an illustration of this in the case of the sailors on the ship with Paul, who fasted two weeks before deliverance came. (Acts 27:33). A most significant fact is that the need of this fast arose because they had failed to heed the Will of God. (Acts 27:21). However, Paul fasted with them. We do not find Bible evidence that extremely long fasts were intended for every one, or even for a large proportion of Christians. It is as the matter of one's becoming a eunuch for the kingdom of heaven's sake: Jesus said that none could receive it save to whom it was given. (Matt. 19:10:12).

On the other hand, we are sure that the evidence warrants that some have obtained great blessings from a protracted fast. Let every man be persuaded in his own mind, and by the extent of his need.

The Place of Medicine and Physicians

Since this book deals specifically with the problems of the believer in the matter of sickness and health, naturally the subject comes up as to the place of medicine and the physician. We do not believe that it is necessary to discuss this matter at length, but we should say that we have always felt that those who attack the doctors have made a serious mistake. The nature of the human body teaches us that there should be those who have special knowledge in teaching people the proper care of it. Surely it is an advantage to have a skilled obstetrician at the birth of a child. A physician who instructs people as to the proper diet is certainly doing an important service. The cities need health departments to administer necessary regulations of sanitation that have vital relation to the public health. Even after the ordinance of Divine healing was given the Children of Israel, the Lord gave certain health laws regarding diet, rest, sanitation, quarantining, etc. Much of the most valuable work of physicians today involves the prevention of disease and the spread of plagues.

Certainly the Bible teaches the care of the sick. The Good Samaritan was commended because he bound up the wounds of the sick, pouring in oil and taking him to a place where he could be cared for. Isaiah told Hezekiah, regarding his healing, to take a fig poultice and apply it to the boil. (Isa. 38:21). The poultice certainly did not heal Hezekiah, but it was good sense to put a poultice upon the boil, and draw off the poison that was exuding. Some who boast that they never go to a doctor, go regularly to a dentist, who is actually a doctor of the teeth.

Having said all this, and freely admitting the good that a physician is able to do, it is quite a different matter when it comes to trusting a physician for one's healing. There is a limit to what a physician can do. He can set a broken bone. He can fill a decayed tooth and thus retard decay. But this work is not really the curing of sickness. When it comes to disease the Christian should go to the Great Physician and get the deliverance provided for. If he is under chastening, it is important that he find the cause and get it out of the way that he might be healed, rather than try to evade God's dealing with him, through the use of medicine and surgery. Alas, how many Christians have leaned on the arm of flesh and in the end it failed them. Asa, King of Judah, was a man who once trusted God when he was in the greatest extremity. But alas in his prosperity he turned from the Lord. When he became sick, instead of seeking God for healing, he sought it at the hand of the physician, *and he died:*

"And Asa in the thirty and ninth year of his reign was diseased in his feet, until his disease was exceeding great: yet in his disease he sought not to the Lord, but to the physicians. And Asa slept with his fathers, and died in the one and fortieth year of his reign." (II Chron. 16:12-13).

Should a person who looks to the Lord for healing take medicine? No one can answer that but the person himself, nor should they. Just stopping the use of medicine will not heal the person. The faith that is born in a man's heart brings the healing. A healed man does not need medicine. The use of any medicine, even as outstanding a one as penicillin, the miracle drug, has an element of uncertainty as to results. Some people are highly allergic to the drug.

It is significant of one woman who had an organic disease and who came to Jesus, that it is said that she "had spent all her living upon physicians, neither could be healed of any." (Luke 8:43). This was not a reflection on physicians. They had done their best, but none could heal her but Jesus. When she touched the hem of His garment, she was healed.

Discerning the Body of Christ

Now as our message draws to a close, let us call to attention one fact that might be overlooked in all that is said. Paul said to those seeking healing, "Let a man examine himself," that he might discern the Lord's body, and not be among those that "are weak and sickly." However, we must never think that because we have done all these things that we are worthy of healing, or that we may base our expectancy of deliverance upon the good works that we have done. No more may a sinner expect to be saved because of good works that he has done. The sinner is expected to turn from his sin, for indeed if he does not, he need not expect salvation; yet his turning from sin is an act that makes available to him the grace of God. So when the afflicted corrects the things that may be resulting in sickness in his body, yet nevertheless he must look for healing through the grace of God which came once and for all through the Atonement of Christ, Who bore our sicknesses upon His own body. "So likewise ye, when ye shall have done all those things which are commanded you, say, We are unprofitable servants: we have done that which was our duty to do." (Luke 17:10).

The fact is that "discerning the Lord's body" is an act of faith. We cannot see the invisible bond of the Lord's Body. We do not see Christ with the natural eye—He is yet in heaven awaiting the hour of His glorious return. The only thing that the natural eye sees is imperfect men and women who nevertheless are His Church. By the eye of faith we see that our own body is a member of that mystical

Body of Christ. Our brothers and sisters are also members of that Body. By faith we discern the Lord's Body.

The secret of the Christian life is the dominion that God places in his spirit over circumstances, evil, oppression, sickness and disease. God originally made man in His own image, and decreed that he should have dominion over the earth. It is a shameful thing to see man shorn of his power, and as Samson of old, bowing before his enemy and grinding in the prison of tormenting sickness. Let him realize his inheritance, that he is a child of the King and Satan has no right nor place in his life. His body is a member of the body of Christ. Let him discern this fact, and repudiate all trace of the enemy's attempted Lordship.

Here is the medicine that a sick person should take. Let him read the 91st Psalm over and over and over until its message sinks in. No plague shall come nigh his dwelling. He shall not fear the pestilence. Ten thousand shall fall at his right hand but it shall not come nigh him. In fact, as the Psalmist declares, no evil shall befall him. Why? Because he dwells in the secret place of God's will. The angels of the Lord encamp around him, lest he dash his foot against a stone. He does not outwit the enemy because of his own brilliance or resourcefulness, but because he has learned to trust implicitly upon his Lord Who has become all in all in his life.

Certainly it is God's will that the Christian should have health for the work that God has given him, and that he should fill out his days in the service of his Lord. Truly God's will for His people in the matter of their health can be expressed no better than the Lord, Himself, expressed it to His redeemed people in the beginning: "And ye shall serve the Lord your God, and he shall bless thy bread, and thy water; and I will take sickness away from the midst of thee." (Exod. 23:25).

www.ingramcontent.com/pod-product-compliance
Lightning Source LLC
LaVergne TN
LVHW011428080426
835512LV00005B/327

*9 7 8 1 9 4 3 8 6 6 3 0 4 *